Bargil Pixner O.S.B.

with Jesus through Galilee
according to the Fifth Gospel

Bargil Pixner O.S.B.

with Jesus through Galilee
according to the
FIFTH GOSPEL

corazin publishing

Translated from German by
Christo Botha
and Dom David Foster,
monk of Downside

© Copyright corazin publishing
Rosh Pina 1992
No part of this book, neither texts nor photos, drawings
or maps, may be copied without written permission
from the publisher
All rights reserved

Printed in Israel

ISBN 965-434-001-1

CONTENTS

PREFACE

In the unfolding of the relationship between God and man there exists not only a progressive History of Salvation but also a Geography of Salvation. God has revealed himself to mankind not only in specific periods of time, but also in very particular places in his creation. The events of the Divine Revelation have flowed into the enormous ocean of the history of mankind, but the places in which God revealed himself to man still remain ever present.

So the soil of the Holy Land as the scene of the events centering around the Person of Jesus can be understood as a Fifth Gospel - as others have already used the term. Whoever has learnt to read and peruse this ›book‹ of biblical landscape will experience the message of the four Gospels with a new and greater clarity. In the opinion of a number of scholars, which is also my own, two of the four Evangelists, namely Mark and John, reveal a profound knowledge of the Galilean landscape which contributes much to the understanding of the development of Jesus' life.

The following study draws mainly from the Gospel of St. Mark. Mark was the first to cast the events in the life of Jesus into the literary form which acquired the name ›gospel‹. This word comes from the Old English ›godspel‹, meaning good tidings, a translation of the Greek ›euangelion‹.

Chronologically speaking, Mark was closest to the circumstances surrounding Jesus's life and gives these historical events a proclamatory character (kerigma). Mark has a distinctive preference for grouping things together according to certain aspects (e.g., the first day in Capernaum or the collection of disputations). One does, on closer inspection, find in his Gospel the succession of various journeys or walks of Jesus through Galilee.

The question whether these successive journeys of Jesus with his disciples through the Galilean country side have a purely redactional character or whether they actually happened as reported, must remain open. I have tried to make the various chapters of this book correspond with the sequence of these journeys. As these unfold, they reflect also an inner development in Jesus himself and in his attitude towards the various social groups (family, kin, the twelve disciples, Pharisees, Essenes, the pagan world and others).

As I am convinced that much of the geographical and historical framework of St. John's Gospel is also based on factual situations, I have occasionally, as a complement, used such data where relevant.

Flavius Josephus, the Jewish historian (ca. AD 38-100), furnished me in various ways with the historical background for the life of Jesus in Galilee. His two major works, The Jewish War (Bellum Judaicum, abbreviation B.J.) and Jewish Antiquities (Antiquitates, abbreviation Ant.), are generally accessible and of extraordinary importance for the understanding of the contemporary history of the New Testament.

I have been living in Israel for more than twenty years and have spent the greater part of the past twelve years at Tabgha by the Sea of Galilee. This has helped me to acquire a certain feel for the land, for distances from one place to another, and for the seasons of drought and of rainfall. Each season has its particular wind-direction, times of heat and cold. I have learnt much about the lake and about fishing and navigation from my Jewish friend Mendel Nun who lives at

Kibbutz Ein Gev. Through his many years of research and experience in fishing its waters, he has become Israel's best known specialist in matters pertaining to the Sea of Galilee. He has also published many studies regarding the topic of fishing as it appears in the Gospels; studies which could well be of great service to biblical scholars. It always strikes the two of us how accurately certain fishing scenes described in the Gospels correspond to the local working methods of fishermen. Even if the various authors of the Gospel were not themselves fishermen, those who have transmitted the oral tradition to them must have had excellent knowledge of fishing methods and of the country side around the lake.

I have also been active as an archaeologist. On Mount Zion in Jerusalem I had the good fortune to uncover the **Gate of the Essenes**, which Flavius Josephus mentions in passing in his description of the Walls of Jerusalem (B.J. 5,145). Here in Galilee I have been active in excavations in Tabgha and have researched many times the hill of Et-Tel, a place which was probably Bethsaida-Julias. Eventually I followed with great interest the excavations started there by Dr. Rami Arav and occasionally joined him in his work. For the past twenty years I have often criss-crossed the whole country with our theology students from Austria, Germany and Switzerland, and have accompanied countless groups of pilgrims in the footsteps of Jesus and introduced them to the homeland of the man, who, 2,000 years ago, proclaimed here the Word of God, the Good News.

Having often been asked to write down the results of my research and my reflections, I find myself now happily in the position to comply with these requests.

I am aware of the problematic nature of such a book. In the last few decades studies of the Gospels have been carried out according to the historical-critical method which has produced important results, but remains rather critical of attempts to reconstruct the life of Jesus. It is often forgotten that behind all exegetical assessment of the Gospel texts there stands a living person: a man, confronted daily with the events of his time and the society in which he lived. Even though noticeable differences exist between Mark's portrayal of Jesus as the Son of God, the Messiah (cf. Mk 1:1) and the Christological testimony as developed by John of a pre-existing Son of God ("The Word became flesh..." Jn 1:14), one should not forget that the event is not itself an editorial invention, but has a historical and geographical background which rests entirely upon given facts.

In the historical-critical exegesis the main emphasis has often been laid on the analysis of particular pericopes or on the identification of particular written sources. The connections between the various Gospel stories are seen mostly as the redactional work of the evangelists. The Evangelist is portrayed as the redactor of a theology particular to a local community.

Attempts to trace a portrait of the historical Jesus as carried out by Life-of-Jesus research (Leben-Jesu-Forschung) are therefore viewed with great skepticism. Such an attitude most certainly has its own justification. However one should not overlook the fact, that many biblical scholars are finding it increasingly difficult to bring to life Jesus' message as a whole. Much effort is spent on the analytical dissection of Gospel texts into the various layers of traditions [Traditionsschichten] and the search for the Christology of the local community where it originated. Hence the attacks of E. Drewermann and the consent that he wins, can also thus be explained. Lately he too seems to be getting ever farther away from the reality of evangelical events.

I hope that this sketch, which springs from a close acquaintance with the landscape of this little corner of Israel may be seen as a modest contribution towards bringing the Man from Galilee closer to the reader. The knowledge of the geography and the contemporary history of two millennia ago makes it clear that the history of a real man is being described and not just the literary construction of an ›Ideal Person‹. One may perhaps dispute the historical validity of some events as described by the evangelists. It should however become clear that the stories in the Gospels often do reflect a great familiarity with the Galilean landscape. Sometimes it cannot be overlooked that the topography receives a ›theological‹ interpretation. But this does not imply that the choice of a certain location must be the arbitrary fabrication of the evangelist.

It is virtually certain that many of the earliest generations of Jewish Christians had first-hand experience of the places described in the Gospel. The excavations in the last few decades of the house of Peter in Capernaum give us clear evidence of the presence of a Jewish Christian community living there for the first four centuries and passing on traditions from father to son. Their local oral traditions, going back to the days of Jesus, were first recorded by the pilgrim Egeria towards the end of the fourth century. Her report of Capernaum and the Seven Springs (Tabgha) is the oldest of its kind. She knows for example of the existence of a place above a cave at the Seven Sources, where *the Lord, as he ascended above it, proclaimed the Beatitudes."*

So when Matthew, for example, mentions the Sermon of Jesus on ›**the Mount**‹, it may very well be an allusion to Mount Sinai. But in view of the local topography it is not at all improbable that Jesus met his disciples on a certain mountain near Capernaum and that crowds gathered around them. Early Christians called that mountain ›Eremos‹, an unpopulated hill, whereto he often withdrew and where he taught. Theology does not need to invent facts; it can easily make use of traditional details, even when these seem to be irrelevant for a particular theological train of thought.

This book largely avoids detailed argumentation. It is intended simply to be a printed form of the story I tried to tell my students and various groups of pilgrims on the site of the events portrayed in the Gospels.

It could nonetheless inspire the critical scholar to re-examine some of those older paths which have long been left untrodden. Incidentally I do hope in the future to present a second book on Jesus of a more serious academic nature, which would include also Jesus' last days in Jerusalem.

Tabgha, at the Sea of Galilee.
Easter Week 1992.

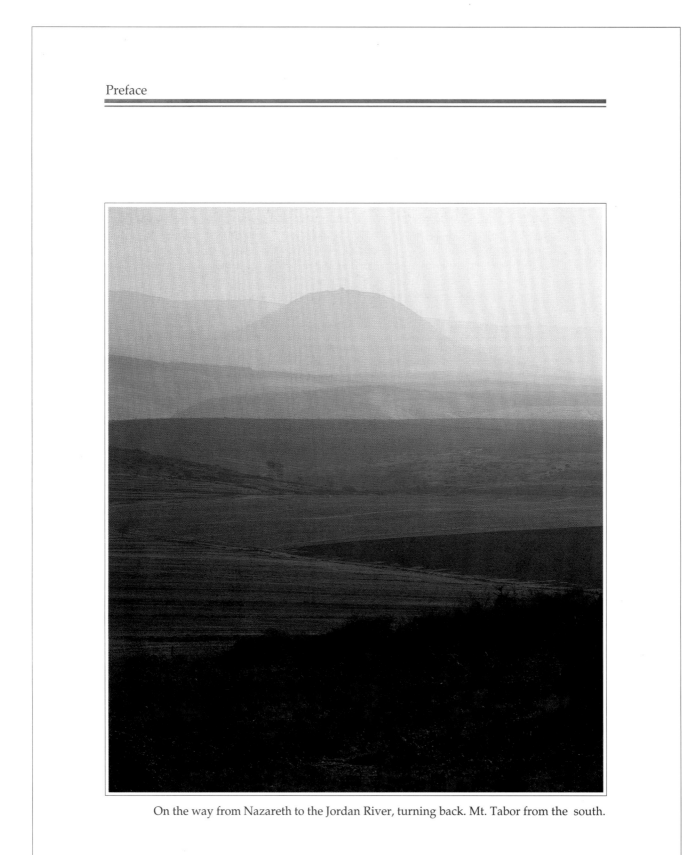

On the way from Nazareth to the Jordan River, turning back. Mt. Tabor from the south.

FROM
NAZARETH
TO THE
JORDAN RIVER

As reported by Mark, Jesus' first journey takes him to John, who is calling his Jewish contemporaries at the Jordan River to a baptism of repentance as preparation for the imminent final Day of Judgement.

"At that time Jesus came from Nazareth in Galilee and was baptized by John in the Jordan." (Mk 1:9) Nazareth was the native town of Jesus. According to Luke the parents of Jesus already lived there before his birth. But Matthew takes a different approach. For him they came to Nazareth only after the return from Egypt. His justification for Nazareth as Joseph's choice for the home of the Messiah sounds rather puzzling. *"And he went and lived in a town called Nazareth. So was fulfilled what was said through the prophets: 'He will be called a Nazarene'* (or Natzorean, in Greek: Nazoraios)." (Mt 2:23)

1. JESUS, THE NATZOREAN

Many conjectures have been made as to which prophetic word Matthew was referring. The great Church father, St. Jerome (A.D. 349-419), who had an excellent knowledge of Hebrew, suggests a very plausible solution. He mentions in his Commentary to this text that many of the Jews who believed in Jesus had a recollection that this word referred to the prophecy of Isaiah 11:1. The word ›shoot‹ (in Hebrew netzer) refers to the scion from the rootstock of Jesse, whose son was King David (cf. PL 52,574). The title Natzorean/Nazarene thus alludes not so much to Jesus' town of origin, but rather denotes his royal descent.

1. **Isaiah 11:1:** *"A shoot will come up from the stump of Jesse, from his roots a Branch* (Hebrew ›netzer‹) *will bear fruit."*

2. **Revelation 22:16b:** *"I* (Jesus) *am the Root and the Offspring of David."*

3. **Jerome:** Commentary on Isaiah (c. 390) on Is. 11:1: *"What all the churchmen seek and do not find in the Prophets, that is, where it stands written: He will be called a Nazarene* (Mt 2:23), *scholars of the Hebrews are of the opinion that it is taken from this passage* (Is. 11:1)" (PL 24,148).

In a letter to Pammachius (c. 395) he cites the above verse like this: *"...and the Nazarene will grow up from his root"* (ep. 57: PL 22,574).

4. According to the **Talmud,** one of five students (talmidim) or teachings (talmudim) of Jesus is called ›netzer‹, relying on Is. 11:1. In its counter citation the Talmud states that this ›netzer‹ should not be linked to Is. 11:1, but to Is. 14:19. *"You are thrown out, out of the grave like a despised shoot"* (Tal. bab., Sanhedrin 43,a).

The blind beggar Bartimaeus sitting by the roadside in Jericho understood it in this way, for when the crowd told him that Jesus of Nazareth (in Greek **ho Nazoraios**, i.e., the Natzorean) was passing by, his spontaneous reaction was: *"Jesus, Son of David, have mercy on me!"* (Mk 10:47; Lk 18:37)

None would assume that the prophecy of Isaiah (11:1) had something to say about that insignificant hamlet in Galilee, nowhere ever mentioned except in the New Testament. The excavations during recent decades have shown that the population of Nazareth at the time of Jesus could hardly have numbered more than 120-150 people. It is most likely that this rather off the beaten track hamlet in the hills of Galilee belonged to the larger village Japhia, just about a mile away, which was a strongly fortified place that played an important role (B.J. 3, 289-306) in the Great War against the Romans (A.D.66-70). During excavations in Caesarea in 1962 a fragment of a marble plaque was discovered with Hebrew inscriptions:

which contained a list of priestly families, who had settled in Galilee during the late Roman era. Among them is mentioned a family in Nazareth. The inscription dates back to 3rd to 4th century A.D. and is the earliest reference to Nazareth in the Jewish epigraphy. It was an important discovery, since it settled an old point of controversy. From the Greek spelling of the word Nazareth it was not clear whether Nazareth was spelled with a ›tz (tzade)‹ or with a ›z (zyne)‹ in Hebrew. The clear ›tz‹ of the Hebrew inscription solved the problem in favor of netzer (shoot, scion). This also eliminates the supposition that the appellation Natzoraios/Nazarene was linked to the name Nazirite (a person consecrated to God, who abstained from fermented drink and let the hair of his head grow long, cf. Nb 6:1-4; Jg 13:5.7) as several early Greek writers, unfamiliar with Hebrew, were prone to believe.

So the designation of Jesus, the Natzorean means in the first place that he was of Davidic lineage rather than that he came from Nazareth. Matthew's prophetic word *"He shall be called a Natzorean"* (2:23) should be taken to refer to Jesus as the netzer-shoot out of the tribe of David.

But can ›netzer‹ also denote a group of people, like a kinship as a whole?

On the basis of the Qumran Scrolls we know that this was in fact the case. From the hymns (psalms) ascribed to the founder of the Qumran-Essenes we see clearly that he refers several times to his Essene community as the ›Netzer-shoot planted by God‹ (1QH vi 15, vii 5,8,10). The Davidic clan from which Jesus originated, must have thought along similar lines. After the death of Jesus the designation Natzoreans, common to Jewish believers gathered around James, the Lord's brother, was later applied to all who belonged to this new religious movement (*"We have found this man to be a troublemaker...he is a ringleader of the Nazarene sect"* Ac 24:5). Even today the Hebrew word for Christians is ›Notzrim‹. The popular expression for the Christians among the Arabs is Nassara.

2. NAZARETH BECOMES POPULATED ONCE AGAIN

One can quite justly assume that Nazara-Nazareth (Little-Netzer) acquired its name from a Davidic clan, that presumably came from Babylon around the year 100 BC. Many examples can be found of tribal or clan names being used to refer to places, e.g., Dan of the tribe of Dan; Shomron(Samaria) from the clan of Shomer; Jebus (Jerusalem) from the Jebusites; Manda, north of Nazareth, in all probability from the clan of the Mandaeans. What the original name of this location of the tribe of Zebulon may have been, is unknown to us. The old settlement reaching back into the Bronze Age was apparently deserted in the year 733 B.C. At that time Tiglath-Pileser III, the Assyrian conqueror, was invading Galilee. He took most of the Israelites into exile to Assyria and created the Assyrian province of Megiddo, replacing the Israelites with peoples of other conquered territories.

So Galilee became a country of gentiles. The Prophet Isaiah regrets the loss of the old tribal areas to paganism: *"In the past he humbled the land of Zebulon and the land of Naphtali."* He calls it the *"Galilee of the Gentiles"* (Isaiah 9:1). But looking into the future, he sees that there a great light will at some time appear.

At the beginning of the Maccabean era (ca. 166 B.C.) only a few isolated Jewish groups were to be found in Galilee. However, this changed dramatically with the conquest of Galilee by the Hasmonaean John Hyrcanus (134-104 B.C.). He as well as his successors Aristobulus I (104-103) and Alexander Jannaeus (103-76) gave the inhabitants a choice: either to accept Judaism by circumcision or to leave the country (Ant.13,310). At the same time a strong immigration (›aliya‹) of Diaspora Jews from Babylon and Persia took place.

The findings of excavations in Nazareth allow conjectures that Nazareth was uninhabited during the Persian and early Hellenistic times (8th - 2nd century B.C.). The lack of any Assyrian, Persian and early Hellenistic ceramic points to a long settlement gap. This absence was confirmed to the author by B. Bagatti, the excavator of Nazareth, shortly before his death in the autumn of 1990. One can surmise that this gap filled when a group of the Davidic Natzorean clan settled in the deserted village as immigrants from the Babylonian exile. Seeing that the Davidic family of Nazareth, as portrayed by the Evangelists, did not only consist of the holy family but also of other clan relatives (syngeneis Mk 6:4), one may well take it for granted that most of the inhabitants of Nazareth belonged to the same extended family, that is to say, to the clan of the Nazarene.

John the Baptist - a Jewish-Christian graffito from the first centuries - found during excavations underneath the Church of Annunciation in Nazareth

This Jewish-Christian ritual bath was found underneath St. Joseph's Church in Nazareth

17

Towards the end of the second century A.D. Julius Africanus, a native of Palestine, tells us that the blood relatives of Jesus (›desposynoi‹ = the Lord's people), in the villages of Kochaba and Nazara, had preserved the Davidic genealogies (cf. Eusebius' citation of Julius Africanus). This geographical distribution of the Davidic clan must have taken place before the beginning of the Christian era. It is known that families of priestly and royal descent laid great store by their genealogies, the former for the validity of their priesthood and the latter on account of the Messianic promises which were tied up with Davidic descent. Kochaba was a village which lay in Batanea (Bashan), a Jewish settlement to the east of the Sea of Galilee and quite near to the pilgrim route from Babylon to Jerusalem. It is most likely, that part of the Nazarene repatriates first settled in Batanea and founded Kochaba (›village of the star‹). A part of this

...the road led down along the Jordan Valley... (Morning mist above the Beth Shean Valley)

clan belonging to the tribe of Judah might have looked for a new home in Galilee, the traditional territory of Zebulon and had given their name to their new village, Nazara (›village of the shoot‹).

3. JESUS WITH JOHN THE BAPTIST

Jesus grew up in Nazareth amidst his tribal brethren, the Natzoreans. When the news reached him that his cousin John was baptizing in the river Jordan near Jericho, he went down there as well, most likely in the company of some members of his family. The road led down into the plain of Jezreel (Esdraelon), past the source of Harod and the city of Beth Shean and down along the Jordan Valley to Jericho. The moment of destiny for Jesus had come. The Spirit of God came upon him as he was immersed in the Jordan waters. That was the impetus for Jesus to relinquish the trade he had hitherto pursued and to follow his new call. The Spirit of God led him into the desert, where a radical and far-reaching change came over him.

John the Baptist made a profound impression on Jesus. John did not only baptize in the southern part of the Jordan, but as Luke tells us, *"went into all the country around the Jordan"* (Lk 3:3). He saw his mission as the preaching of the baptism of repentance, a preacher wandering in the spirit of Elijah. It is striking that he visited precisely the places which were strongly linked with Elijah. For example he preached at the Jordan near Jericho, where *"Elijah went up to heaven in a whirlwind"* (2K 2:11-12) in a chariot of fire. He also baptized at Aenon near Salim (Jn 3:23), which was located south of Bet-Shean near Mehola, where Elijah *"threw his cloak around"* Elisha, his successor (1K 16:19). Earlier Jesus had met John in Bethany beyond the Jordan (Jn 1:28). It is the place by the river, where Elijah hid in the *"Kerith Ravine, east of the Jordan,"* to be safe from the wrath of King Ahab and where Elijah was fed by a raven (1K 17:3ff). The location of this old tradition is related by Egeria (c. 384) in the report of her travel to the grave of Job, which she was looking for in the Batanea. Thus the name ›Nahal Kerit‹ must be identified with the river, which in Hellenistic times had acquired the Greek name Yarmuk (hieros muchos, i.e,. Holy Ravine). According to a new, well-founded interpretation, this Bethany beyond the Jordan where Jesus found his first disciples, is identical to the Batanea where, as we have seen, the Kochaba of the Natzorean clan lay.

We can only guess where Jesus went after that fateful event of his baptism in the Jordan. *"The Spirit immediately drove him out into the wilderness"* (Mk 1:12). Were the bare ravines of the Judean desert the scene where Satan dazzled the mind of Jesus with the various possibilities of trying out the newly discovered power of his divine sonship? Seeking the will of his Father by means of prayer and fasting, he dismissed such presumption by his decisive rebuke, *"Away from me, Satan!"* (Mt 4:10). Having resisted the temptation in the desert he felt the need to go once more to John the Baptist.

This is the meeting of which the Fourth Gospel informs us. It does not report Jesus' baptism, although it assumes it as having taken place. *"Then John gave this testimony: 'I saw the Spirit come down from heaven as a dove and remain on him'"* (Jn 1:32). John was baptizing at a tributary of the Jordan in the far northeast of the Judean country. The territory of Bashan, later called Batanea or Basanitis, was originally the ancestral territory of the tribe of Manasseh and belonged at the time of Herod the Great (37-4 B.C.) to Judea. Today it is in the southwest corner of Syria. The pilgrim's route from Babylon to Jerusalem ran past it. In order to keep this route free from bandits who threatened it, Herod offered the possibility of settling there to a Judean clan which had come from Babylon and under the leadership of Zamaris was looking for a new home. They named the region of settlement after the Persian capital Ekbatana and founded a stronghold at Bathyra. Because they were successful in bringing peace to the whole region of the Batanea and since the region was also taxfree many Jews moved there, who, as Josephus reported, *"observed the laws of the Fathers (therapeyetai)"* (Ant. 17,26). It is quite likely that groups of the Essenes were to be found amongst these devout Jews.

Coin minted under Herod's reign

These Babylonian Jews excelled as skilful horsemen and soldiers and were charged with the responsibility of training the mercenary armies of the Herodian kings. So it is not surprising that soldiers also came to John the Baptist, who was baptizing *"at Bethany on the other side of the Jordan"* (cf Lk 3:14.12). These soldiers had a particular sympathy for John the Baptist, which was destined to become the undoing of his murderer Herod Antipas (cf Ant. 18, 114.116). Jesus stayed in John's neighborhood for a while, and some of John's disciples began to follow Jesus.

When John the Baptist saw Jesus coming towards him, he drew the attention of two of his disciples to him as the one who was to come after him *"This is the one I meant when I said, 'A man who comes after me has surpassed me because he was before me'"* (Jn 1:30). The two followed

Jesus and put to him the question *"'Rabbi,' (which means Teacher),' where are you staying?' 'Come,' he replied, 'and you will see.' So they went and saw where he was staying, and spent that day with him"* (Jn 1:38b.39). Can we suppose that Jesus was then staying with members of his kinship in Kochaba? The first four disciples Andrew, Peter, Philip and John who had met Jesus as members of the circle around John the Baptist all came from Bethsaida, which was only half a day's journey away.

Nathanael met the small group of new disciples who were travelling with Jesus when they were passing Bethsaida on their way to the wedding at Cana. He came from Cana in Galilee, only a few hours' walk to the north of Nazareth. When this *"true Israelite"* (Jn 4:47) heard from his friend Philip that Jesus was from Nazareth, Nathanael rather pertly replied: *"Nazareth! Can anything good come from there?"* (Jn 1:46) He was actually trying to express his skepticism: Could anything worthwhile come forth from that dump on the hills, from those clannish little people, who so self-conceitedly fancied themselves to be of so-called royal descent?

But when he met Jesus for himself and witnessed the miracle on the third day (Jn 2:1) at the wedding in Cana, his initial contempt for Jesus changed into enthusiasm. Jesus, the Nazarene, *"thus revealed his glory, and his disciples put their faith in him"* (Jn 2:11).

4. ADVENT MOOD

After the wedding Jesus left Cana with his newly-won friends for Capernaum by the Lake. Was this a goodwill visit to the native country of his future Apostles? Did Jesus prefer to meet their families first, before selecting his disciples? The fourth Gospel tells us about the rubbing of shoulders between the family of the Natzorean and the followers of John the Baptist: *"After this he went down to Capernaum with his mother and brothers and his disciples. There they stayed for a few days"* (Jn 2:12).

When the Feast of Passover A.D. 28 was approaching Jesus made his way to the Holy City of Jerusalem, no doubt accompanied by his brothers and some of the followers of John the Baptist. Here, according to John, the event known as the Cleansing of the Temple took place. This event drew the attention of many to Jesus. Among these may have been people belonging to circles of Essenes; they regarded the temple priesthood of that time as illegal and the sacrifices as illegitimate.

What happened next in the summer months following that Passover? John tells us that Jesus operated for a time in the fellowship of John the Baptist, but farther away to the south in Judea (Jn 3:22). The distinctive feature of this period was his readiness to baptize people, of which we later hear no more. It is also quite clear that as long as he adhered to this practice Jesus must have been regarded by the public as a follower of John the Baptist. Many may have regarded him as the acknowledged favorite of John the Baptist and his most successful missionary. In this sense Jesus' early activity can be regarded as an episode in the movement started by John the Baptist and not yet as belonging to the distinctive ministry of Jesus himself. We can therefore distinguish three stages in the development of baptism:

1. *Baptism of oneself* in running (living) water ›Mikveh‹ in order to gain ritual purity, as practiced by the Essenes.

2. The *Plunging* into running water by a Baptizer as a sign of conversion and repentance in preparation for the kingdom of God.

3. *Christian baptism* as an effective sign of entry into God's kingdom.

While John the Baptist was baptizing at Aenon near Salim (situated near the middle section of the course of the river Jordan (Jn 3:23), *"the Pharisees heard that Jesus was gaining and baptizing more disciples than John, although in fact it was not Jesus who baptized, but his disciples. When the Lord learned of this, he left Judea and went back once more to Galilee. Now he had to go through Samaria"* (Jn 4:1-4).

He reached it by the ancient mountain road, which follows more or less the watershed between the Mediterranean Sea and the Jordan Valley. He passed near Bethel, where Jacob, the patriarch, *"had a dream in which he saw a ladder resting on the earth, with its top reaching to heaven, and the angels of God were ascending and descending on it"* (Gen 28:12). He passed to the east of Elasa, where Judas the Maccabee had fallen. He hurried across the notorious Valley of the Robbers and reached Shiloh, the original site of the resting place of the Ark of the Covenant, where Samuel was called to become God's prophet. Exhausted by their journey, the group with Jesus would finally reach Jacob's well at Sychar. Here the conversation with the Samaritan woman took place (Jn 4:1-26).

This is already an indication that the Messianic kingdom would not remain restricted to the Jewish people but extend beyond it. The Samaritans, with whom Jesus stayed for two days, sensed something of this widening of horizons. *"We no longer believe just because of what you said; now we have heard for ourselves, and we know that this man really is the Saviour of the world"* (Jn 4:42).

By including this account John the Evangelist undoubtedly wanted to legitimize the missionary work among the Samaritans, which was undertaken by the early Church soon after the outpouring of the Holy Spirit at Pentecost. After his two days in Samaria Jesus continued his journey to his native country. *"When he arrived in Galilee, the Galileans welcomed him. They had seen all that he had done in Jerusalem at the Passover Feast, for they also had been there"* (Jn 4:45).

However the initial enthusiasm was not to last long, as incidents soon to take place in Nazareth would show. *"Now Jesus himself had. pointed out that a prophet has no honor in his own country"* (Jn 4:44).

JESUS COMES TO CAPERNAUM

1. THREE TORAH SCHOOLS

Three large Jewish schools of learning existed during Jesus' lifetime. Each one had its own opinion about how the Torah, the Law of Moses, the fundamental law of Israel, should be interpreted and made use of in daily life.

Politically the most influential school was that of the SADDUCEES.

The Sadducees were composed largely of the priestly aristocracy. They laid particular store by the Temple cult and regarded only the five Books of Moses as the Word of God, and not the Books of the Prophets. They also rejected belief in the resurrection of the dead. They held that God rewarded the just already in this life.

Of different opinion were the ESSENES. The original nucleus of this deeply religious movement was a group of priests under the leadership of the ›Teacher of Righteousness‹, who withdrew from the Temple service into the desert around the middle of the second century B.C. They regarded the Maccabean (Hasmonean) high priests,

who invested themselves with royal powers, as usurpers, and their sacrificial offerings in the Temple as illegitimate. To purify themselves from guilt they no longer offered sacrifices but purified themselves in ritual baths. Judging from the Copper Scroll they had three monastic centers, called ›kokhlit‹, one at Secacah (the ruins of Qumran), another on the southwestern hill of Jerusalem (present-day Zion) and a third in ›the Land of Damascus‹ (in the corner formed by the rivers Yarmuk and Rukkad (in modern southern Syria).

What distinguished them more than anything else from the other groups was their special solar calendar, which they considered genuine, while the calendar used in the Temple they abhorred as having been adulterated by pagan influences. Their own calendar counted exactly 52 weeks in a year of 364 days. So Passover and the Feast of Tabernacles, for instance, would always fall on a Wednesday. According to Philo and Flavius Josephus, unmarried as well as married Essenes were to be found in most towns and villages of the country. John the Baptist probably belonged to this movement, but left it to pursue his own mission. The Natzorean clan might possibly have been influenced by them.

Third and most important was the school of the PHARISEES. Like the Essenes they originally belonged to the Hasidic movement, only to separate themselves (Perushim - Pharisee = the Separated) to develop their own ›Halakhah‹, i.e., Way of the Torah. They maintained that the collection of their ›Oral Ancestral Traditions‹ went back to Moses himself. They were especially concerned to safeguard observance of the Divine Law by creating a multitude of secondary laws, that formed a hedge around the Torah. The Writings of the Prophets were regarded by them as the word of God. They believed in the resurrection of the dead at the end of time. Their most famous teachers were the benevolent and wise Rabbi Hillel and the strict Shammai. They earned themselves great credit for strengthening the Jewish consciousness, especially in Galilee, where the population consisted largely of Jews, whose parents or grandparents converted during the

Hasmonean policy of compulsory Judaization. Their numbers were reinforced by immigration from the Babylonia.

Of these three religious movements, only the school of the Pharisees has survived among the Jewish people until today and is the foundation of rabbinic Judaism. At the time of Jesus, however, all three movements were recognized forms of Jewish life. Flavius Josephus, for example, who came from a priestly Sadducean family, belonged at some stage of his life to one or other of the three schools. All three recognized the Torah as supreme law, but each group had its own Halakhah, i.e., interpretation, how the law should be observed.

As we shall see later, there are reasons to believe that the Natzorean clan, and so also Jesus' family, was influenced by the school of the Essenes. In addition, Mary was related to Elizabeth, daughter and wife of priests. Zechariah and John the Baptist were both Kohanim, i.e., priests (cf. Lk 1:5).

2. THE ARRIVAL OF JESUS AT THE LAKE

After Jesus had been baptized by John in the Jordan near Jericho and spent some time with him in Bethany (Jn 1:28) he remained for several months in the fellowship of the Baptist. While Jesus was active somewhere in Judea accompanied by individual followers of John the Baptist, the latter himself worked at Aenon near Salim. According to the account of the pilgrim Egeria c. 384 A.D. (see box p. 107) this place can be identified as Tel Salim, approximately eight miles south of the city of Beth Shean and about one mile west of the Jordan. Aenon was the area of *"the abundant waters"* (Jn 3:23), which rise near Tel Salim. The Israelis today call it ›Ainot Mechatzetzim‹ and the rich springs supply large fish ponds. John tells us *"there was plenty of water, and people were constantly coming to be baptized. This was before John was put in prison. An argument developed between some of John's disciples and a certain Jew over the matter of ceremonial washing. They came to John and said to him, 'Rabbi, that man who was with you on the other side of the Jordan - the one you testified about - well, he is baptizing, and everyone is going to him'"* (Jn 3: 23-26).

27

It was on this occasion that John gave his jealous partisans the splendid reply: *"He must become greater; I must become less."*(Jn 3:30).

...John himself worked at Aenon near Salim... .(The Springs of Aenon, with Tel Salim)

The former disciples of John the Baptist who had joined Jesus continued to preach and baptize precisely in the same manner as John (cf. Jn 3:22). It was a baptism in preparation for the coming of God's Kingdom. They came and left their new teacher Jesus just as they had done with John. At that time Jesus had still not begun to exercise his own ministry.

But then came the turning-point. Herod Antipas threw John the Baptist into prison. Jesus recognized that the time for him to act had come. This is where Mark takes up the thread of the story (Mk 1,14). Matthew is even more explicit: *"When Jesus heard that John had been put in prison, he returned to Galilee. Leaving Nazareth, he went and lived in Capernaum, which was by the lake in the area of Zebulun and Naphtali - to fulfill what was said through the prophet Isaiah"* (Mt 4:12-14). The region had been subjected to 600 years of pagan occupation and now after

View towards the Valley of the Doves

130 years of renewed Jewish consciousness the time had come for the area by the lake to see the ›great light‹ of which Isaiah had spoken (Isaiah 9:1-25).

On his way from Nazareth to Capernaum Jesus passed Sepphoris (Zippori), which lies slightly to the north of Nazareth. Sepphoris used to be the capital of Galilee but had recently had to surrender that honor to the newly established Tiberias. Jesus then by-passed Cana, which lies at the foot of Mt. Asamon and walked along the plain of Azotis (Beit Netofa). At Nimra (today Kh. Amudim: some columns of the old synagogue have remained) he crossed a lower pass and descended through the Valley of the Doves (Wadi Hamam) towards the Lake. At the end of the Valley of the Doves he was able to quench his thirst at the so-called ›Spring of the Apostles‹, which lies at the foot of Mt. Arbel with its magnificent rocky face. In its caves the opponents of Herod the Great had taken refuge, but they were tracked down and annihilated ruthlessly. In Magdala, called Tarichaea ›dried fish‹ in the Greek, Jesus reached the high road, the Via Maris. Passing Gennesaret at the foot of the ruins of Kinneret, the former capital of the tribe of Naphtali, Jesus came to Heptapegon, the fishing ground of Capernaum's fishermen. This place with the Canaanite name of Magadan, which probably meant ›the Waters of Gad‹ or maybe ›Waters of Good Luck‹, was called in Greek Heptapegon, ›the Seven Springs‹, a word Arab tongues later shortened to Tabgha.

In winter and in spring the fish, who are looking for warmth, especially the tropical Peter's fish, which suffer from the cold, are attracted to the warm water of the springs rising at the foot of the Eremos hill and flowing into the lake. This attraction is fatal to the fish, for it offers the fishermen the opportunity to make abundant catches.

Abundant catches of fish!

3. THE CALLING OF THE TWO PAIRS OF BROTHERS

Here Jesus may have thought that he could most easily find once again the disciples that he had already met in the company of John the Baptist in Batanea on the other side of the Jordan (cf. Jn 1:28). These fishermen had apparently returned to their trade. It seems as though Jonah, the father of Andrew and Simon and Zebedee, together

...a joint fishing business...

with his sons James and John, had already conducted a joint fishing business for some time (cf. Lk 5:10). According to old sources both fishing families came from Bethsaida, situated near the mouth of the river Jordan. Bethsaida could be translated as ›House of Fishing‹ (Fishington). It was a large town in the territory of Gaulanitis whose ruler Herod Philip bestowed upon it the rank of city (polis). Simon the fisherman from Bethsaida had met his wife in Capernaum and lived then with his brother in the house of his mother-in-law (cf. Mk 1:30). Both families maintained friendly relations and continued their joint business. They had gone fishing in a large boat which they shared. While Zebedee, together with his sons and their hired men, was preparing the large draw nets for the next catch, Simon and Andrew were fishing on their own somewhat to the west. Standing in the shallow water of the Magadan shore (Tabgha), they threw their cast-nets into the lake with great dexterity .

That is when Jesus passed by. He noticed the two brothers and called them into his fellowship. *"'Come, follow me,' Jesus said, 'and I will make you fishers of men.'"* (Mk 1:17). He wanted to say, "Friends, John (the Baptist) is languishing in the prison of Machaerus fortress, far

31

away by the Dead Sea. Now the time has come, *the kingdom of God is near*" (Mk 1:15). *"At once they left their nets and followed him. When he had gone a little farther, he saw James son of Zebedee and his brother John in a boat, preparing their nets"* (Mk 1:18-19). East of the present-day Chapel of Mensa Christi in Tabgha is a little harbor, called the Harbor of Peter. Behind it a very strong current of water enters the lake cascading from the ›Source of Capernaum‹. Fishermen of old could easily wash their nets there. Jesus called these two brothers to be his followers as well. And so the five of them walked the two miles to Capernaum. After the two pairs of brothers had gone, the father Zebedee was left with his hired men. Together they pulled in the nets and continued fishing.

So Mark describes Jesus' arrival in Capernaum, which was to become his adopted home. It seems as though in Capernaum Jesus freed himself more and more from the Essene influence of his clan. The narrow outlook of the Essene circles which focussed exclusively on their own group became too narrow and exclusive for Jesus' liking. During his days in Capernaum he inclined increasingly towards the ideas of the Pharisees. They were concerned for the whole people. During Jesus' first stay in Jerusalem he had won the friendship of a *"man of the Pharisees named Nicodemus"* (Jn 3:1), a man of Galilean descent, a friend who, at least in secret, remained true to him to the bitter end.

Jesus took much over from Rabbi Hillel's school and he was rather negative and disapproving of the school of Shammai. Among the Pharisees he had many friends and sympathizers. Later he visited Simon the Pharisee (cf. Lk 7:36). It seems that the disputes and the conflict stories also were to a large extent arguments between various groups of Pharisees. Jesus' attacks against the Pharisees were often over-accentuated by the four evangelists because of later historical developments.

The distance between Jesus and the influence of his family and clan was ever increasing. He began to build his own spiritual family in the form of a Pharisee Khavura (circle of friends) in which he was the Rabbi, surrounded by his twelve disciples as the khaverim.

...a very strong current of water ...from the ›Source of Capernaum.‹..

EVER
WIDER
CIRCLES

1. CAPERNAUM, HIS TOWN

Capernaum became Jesus' adopted home. In all probability Jesus had no house there that he could call his own. He said of himself, *"Foxes have holes and birds of the air have nests; but the Son of Man has nowhere to lay his head"* (Mt 8:20). He lived with Peter. Recent excavations seem to confirm this. The house of Peter was a century-old house, but since Jesus and Peter had lived there it had been venerated by the Jewish believers, who had scribbled both their names onto the walls and these graffiti could still in part be deciphered. Capernaum was the place from where Jesus started his travels and to which he always returned. His field of activity was concentrated more in the countryside along the northwestern shore of the lake, the so-called ›Evangelical Triangle‹.

Matthew refers to Capernaum, Korazin and Bethsaida as the cities *"in which most of his miracles had been performed"* (Mt 11:20). In addition there was the local mountain of Capernaum, in fact a ridge of hills just to the west of the town. This ridge is the one referred to in the Gospels as the solitary place ›eremos topos‹ or as **the mountain** (cf. Mt 28:16, Mk 6:46). Ancient tradition (Egeria) named this hillcrest ›Eremos‹ (cf. the letter of Abbot Valerian). At the foot of Eremos lies the

Even before the arrival of its green leaves, the urginea sends forth its long, white blossoms. This is a sign that the first rain and the life giving winter season are near. (View from Eremos to the Harbor of Peter)

area of springs which carried the name Ma-gadan (Heptapegon). The line Tabgha-Eremos-Korazin forms one side of the triangle, the second stretches from Korazin along the still recognizable Roman road towards Bethsaida, situated on a hillock on the other side of the Jordan. The lake shore from the mouth of the Jordan as far as Tabgha forms the base of the triangle. Capernaum, his own town, (in Matthew's words: *"Jesus stepped into a boat, crossed over and came to his own town"* Mt 9:1), lies in the middle of the base of the triangle.

Capernaum was a frontier town, not far from the Jordan and had, according to the latest estimates, between 1,000 and 1,500 inhabitants. A garrison of mercenary soldiers under the supervision of a centurion was also stationed there. They served Herod Antipas. The mercenaries were probably not Romans, but might have been recruited from Phrygia, Gaul or Germany. They protected the frontier, provided back-up for the tax collectors, who had to collect the prescribed duties and generally saw to public order. One of the duties of the publicans was to collect the dues for the fish caught in the lake, whose owner was the king. The custom house of the publican, Matthew, must have stood some place where the Via Maris passed close by the lake shore on the outskirts of the town.

Recent excavations have shown that this military garrison had its quarters to the east of the Jewish village. The troops lived in better houses than the local population. To everybody's surprise the excavations showed, that these soldiers had a typical Roman bath (with caldarium, tepidarium and frigidarium, etc.) at their disposal. Such findings shed new light on the scene of the centurion of Capernaum (Mt 8:5-13; Lk 7:1-10). This man must have been a very able and responsible official, who maintained good relations with his Jewish neighbors. The elders of the Jews told Jesus that *"he loves our nation and has built our synagogue"* (Lk 7:5). *"This man deserves to have you do this."* This officer displayed a remarkable sensitivity for the Jewish inhabitants when he considered himself unworthy to receive the Jewish Rabbi Jesus into his Gentile home. The centurion therefore gave Jesus to understand that the latter could certainly heal his servant from afar. Jesus is pleasantly surprised. *"I tell you, I have not found such great faith even in Israel"* (Lk 7:9).

2. GALILEAN SPRINGTIME

After the winter rains when the countryside around the lake is clothed in the green of springtime, buds in thousands burst open in the warm sun. On hills and in valleys vegetation puts forth shoots

EGERIA was a pilgrim who belonged to a circle of pious women in Spain. She wrote for them an extensive account of her three-year stay in the lands of the Bible (between ca. 383 and 395). The major part of this account has survived. Parts which were lost from the original work have come to us through copyists. One of these was the Benedictine monk Peter the Deacon, librarian of Monte Cassino. We owe to him Egeria's description of Capernaum and Tabgha. The local traditions which she picked up go back to the Jewish Christian inhabitants of Capernaum.

"In Capernaum, a church was made out of the house of the prince of the Apostles, the walls of which are standing to this day just as they were. That is where the Lord healed the paralytic (cf. Mk 2:2-12).

The synagogue is also there, in which the Lord healed the possessed man (cf. Mk 1:23-26). *The visitor climbs up to it by several steps; this synagogue is built out of squared blocks of masonry.*

Not far from there the stone steps can be seen on which the Lord stood (cf. Jn 21:4).

Above the Lake there is also a field of grass with much hay and several palms. By it are the SEVEN SPRINGS, each of which supplies a huge quantity of water. In the field the Lord fed the people with five loaves of bread (cf. Mk 6:31-44).

The Stone on which the Lord placed the bread has been made into an altar. Visitors take small pieces of rock from this stone for their welfare and it brings benefit to everyone.

Along the walls of the church runs the public highway where the apostle Matthew sat to collect taxes (cf. Mk 2:13-14).

On the hill which rises nearby is a grotto, upon which the Lord ascended when he taught the Beatitudes (cf. Mt 5:1).

(D. BALDI, Enchiridion Locorum Sanctorum, Jerusalem (1982) 281, nr 412 and 290, nr 443)

and blossoms, and the human heart expands in response to such beauty. The first months of Jesus' public activity may be compared to such a springtime.

In the account of her visit to Capernaum and Tabgha (ca. 383) the pilgrim Egeria recorded a tradition, which may well go back to the Jewish-Christians of Capernaum. She tells of a cave in the hillside at the Seven Springs (Ma-gadan, Tabgha), "and the Lord ascending above it preached the Beatitudes." The terrace above this still existing cave, called Mughara Ayub, must be considered the traditional place of the Sermon on the Mount. The hillcrest of Eremos indeed offers a magnificent view over the entire lake and the surrounding villages. The cragginess of this hill meant it was left uncultivated and enabled Jesus to gather large crowds around him without causing damage to the farmers. It is joy to the heart to see everything turning green and blossoming during springtime on the Eremos heights. It must have been the red anemones and the blue iris that inspired Jesus to reflect on the *lilies of the field* (Mt 6:28) whose beauty surpasses that of *Solomon's in all its splendor* (Mt 6:29).

Eremos – Mount of Beatitudes

Blessed

are the poor in spirit,
for theirs is the kingdom of heaven.

Blessed

are those who mourn,
for they will be comforted.

Blessed

are the meek,
for they will inherit the earth.

Blessed

are those who hunger and thirst for righteousness,
for they will be filled.

Blessed

are the merciful,
for they will be shown mercy.

Blessed

are the pure in heart,
for they will see God.

Blessed

are the peacemakers,
for they will be called sons of God.

Blessed

are those who are persecuted because of
righteousness,
for theirs is the kingdom of heaven.

The friendliness of this region has undoubtedly influenced the character of the Good News which Jesus proclaimed here. The law of the Old Covenant, which had in the background the mighty Jebel Musa, Mount Sinai, with its rugged rocks of red granite and naked wind-swept cliffs, has a much harsher tone to it than the Gospel which went forth from this mountain. The Eremos hill with its array of blossom, its birdsong and its splendid view over the lake - the Arabs call it ›God's Eye‹ - became the Mountain of the New Covenant, the Mount of the Beatitudes.

Mark narrates that in the beginning of his ministry Jesus withdrew to Eremos (›solitary place‹) to pray after that first eventful day in Capernaum. Peter went to look for him in the small hours of the day and found Jesus there: *"Everyone is looking for you!"* (Mk 1:37).

At this point Matthew inserts the Sermon on the Mount. Having mentioned the fact that the tidings of Jesus' teaching and activities had spread as far as Syria (*"News about him spread all over Syria, and people brought to him all who were ill"* Mt 4:24), he enumerates the various regions from where the crowds came streaming: *"Large crowds from Galilee, the Decapolis, Jerusalem, Judea and the region across the Jordan followed him"* (Mt 4:25).

The start of Jesus' public activity is characterized by the throng of people, who listened to him enraptured, *"because he taught as one who had authority, and not as their teachers of the law"* (Mt 7:29).

The Sermon on the Mount is a summary of the fundamental teaching of Jesus. It starts with the proclamation of the eight Beatitudes and Matthew devotes three whole chapters of his Gospel to it.

Jesus is fully aware of his own authority and develops here his own Halakhah based on the Torah and thus puts himself in opposition to the Pharisees and Essenes alike. As a fundamental and divine Law the Torah remains irreversible. *"Do not think that I have come to abolish the Law or the Prophets; I have not come to abolish them but to fulfill them"* (Mt 5:17-19).

Repeatedly it says: "You have heard that it was said..." and each time Jesus makes an alteration: "But I tell you..."

Jesus envisages a different attitude towards our fellow human beings.

His remarks hit the Pharisees directly, the Essenes indirectly. The latter divided mankind into two categories: God's friends and his enemies. The one they referred to as the ›Sons of the Light‹ and the other ›Sons of the Darkness‹. The former were to be loved, the latter to be hated. That was the Essene halakhah and had nothing to do with the Torah. *"You have heard that it was said, 'Love your neighbor and hate your enemy.' But I tell you: Love your enemies and pray for those who persecute you, that you may be sons and daughters of your Father in heaven. He causes his sun to rise on the evil and the good, and sends rain on the righteous and the unrighteous"* (Mt 5:43). No more will it be an "Eye for an eye, and a tooth for a tooth", but rather "Love your enemies!"

The Mosaic rule of compensation was not based on revenge, but rather on just recompense. The evildoer should repay only to the extent of his wrongdoings. Evil should be combatted but Jesus sees this in a different way. Jesus seems to demand the rejection of the natural human impulses to revenge. This is provocatively original. In the kingdom of God the law of love and not of revenge should rule. A love that excludes nobody.

After his sermon on the Eremos-heights Matthew has Jesus go down to the lake. A leper approaches Jesus and begs to be healed. According to the Jewish prescription a person cured of leprosy had to take a ritual bath. The healed man may have done this right on the spot. For this reason the most easterly Tabgha spring was designated as the ›Bath of the Leper‹.

The Byzantines enclosed this spring with a round tower, which still stands. In Muslim tradition the ›Bath of the Leper‹ itself got healing power. The leper, though, was no longer the man cured by Jesus, but the patient Job (in Arabic Ayub), who was said to have been healed of his leprosy after bathing seven times in these waters. The Moslems and especially the Druse still use this bath (Hamam Ayub) as a source of healing.

40

The ›Bay of the Parables‹

3. THE SERMON FROM THE BOAT

Once again Mark tells us of large crowds that gathered around Jesus (Mk 3:7). They pressed round him by the lakeside. *"The crowd that gathered round him was so large that he got into a boat and sat in it out on the lake, while all the people were along the shore at the water's edge. He taught them many things by parables"* (Mk 4:1-2). For the location of this off-shore sermon local tradition points to a distinctive bay which lends a vivid and suitable background to the story. The bay or inlet, also called ›Bay of the Parables‹, lies half-way between Tabgha and Capernaum. The land slopes down like an Roman theater around the bay. Even today this natural formation possesses astonishing acoustics, which have been scientifically investigated by the Israelis. It has been proven that Jesus' voice could have carried effortlessly from his floating pulpit to a crowd of several thousand people on the shore. In his first parable Jesus spoke about the seed being sown by the sower. One part thereof *"fell along the path, some fell on rocky places or fell among thorns and still other seed fell on good soil"* (Mk 4:4,5,7-8). Jesus' audience found themselves sitting in exactly the right setting to be able to vividly imagine what he was saying: along the road to Capernaum there is much rocky ground and plenty of thorns and thistles can be seen. Moreover, the black earth, a product of the disintegration of lava (basalt), is particularly fertile.

4. HAZARDOUS CROSSING

What prompted Jesus on the evening after the Sermon by the Lake to say, *"Let us go over to the other side"* (Mk 4:35)? Was it missionary zeal suddenly awakened or a deliberate challenge to the powers of the underworld? The steep cliffs of the Hippene, the most northern part of the Decapolis, loomed menacingly from afar. The city Hippos (in Aramaic ›Susita‹) lay there like a fortress on the basalt plateau, resembling the head of a noble steed and looking defiantly across to Tiberias, her rival on the other side of the lake. A number of smaller villages were lying around Hippos like little chicks gathered around the mother hen. Kursi, a fishing village in the northwestern corner of the Hippene, as the region was called, was one of the villages over which the city of Hippos held dominion. There Jesus' boat was heading with other boats in its wake.

What did the Jewish prophet want in this pagan area where Satan reigned supreme? Mark, who again and again portrays Jesus as the challenger of demons, sharply intimates the suspense. He wrote this pericope at a time when the Gospel was having great difficulty in taking root in the pagan world. To him as well as to his Jewish contemporaries the cult of idols was a mere facade for the demoniac.

Exhausted by the day's work Jesus lay down to rest, his head on a pillow in the back of the boat, and soon he fell asleep. Suddenly the powers of the underworld launched their attack to prevent this dangerous man from breaking into their realm. A tremendous storm sprang up to drown this venture in the waters of the Gennesaret. Awakened by the frightened apostles Jesus rose up and took charge.
As in earlier exorcisms he threatened the wind (cf. Mk 1:25) and he rebuked the evil spirit of chaos: *"'Quiet! Be still!' Then the wind died down and it was completely calm"* (Mk 4:39).

The first obstacle had no sooner been overcome, when the second one was already in store. *"They went across the lake to the region of the Gerasenes. When Jesus got out of the boat, a man with an evil spirit came from the tombs to meet him"* (Mk 5:1).

With his vivid description of the possessed man Mark depicts the depravity of paganism, but also its formidable strength. The man under the power of the evil spirits cries out, "Leave me alone! Have you come here to torture me?" The demons must acknowledge the higher authority of the Son of Man; that they carry the name ›Legion‹ is perhaps an allusion to the Roman legions with whose help Pompey had founded the Decapolis. Pompey came from Syria in 63 B.C. and conferred pagan-hellenistic city rights on the Decapolis. Because of these legions the demons insist that they have the right to remain in this region, if not in people, at least in the pigs.

Why pigs? The Canaanites had sacrificed pigs to the demons. The archaeologists have found altars erected for that purpose. In the Canaanite period all slaughtering of animals was in a way a sacrifice. So this special relationship between pigs and demons becomes understandable. Moreover the emblem of one of the most famous legions, the Decima Fretensis, was that of the wild boar (cf. also Is 65:48).

Mark continues his narrative: *"A large herd of pigs was feeding on the nearby hillside"* (Mk 5:11). Matthew specifies: *"Some distance from them a large herd of pigs was feeding"* (Mt 8:30). According to a description by Origen it has been suggested that this hillside could have been just south of Kursi, where the rocky precipice drops suddenly down to the lake.Wherever and however the evangelical scene might have taken place, the attempt of the demons ended in an act of total self-destruction and banishment of the evil one into the eerie depths of the lake. In vivid colors Mark portrays the collision between the kingdom of God and the kingdom of Satan.

The idea that this corner of the gentile Decapolis was under the spell of the powers of darkness also influenced later generations. In order to overcome such nefast influence the Byzantines built a monastery in Kursi.

In **Ezekiel 39:11** we read:
"On that day I will give Gog a burial place in Israel, in the valley of those passing by on the east of the Sea. It will block the way of the travelers, because Gog and all his hordes will be buried there. So it will be called the Valley of Hamon Gog."
This prophecy of the apocalyptic battle of the armies of Israel against the evil forces of Gog and Magog seemed to apply to Wadi Semakh (›Hamon-Gog‹), at the entrance of which lay Kursi, ›on the east of the Sea‹ of Galilee. During the "dark" Middle Ages the notion made its rounds that the "Antichrist" would be born in that region.

5. THE EXPELLED BECOME EXPELLERS

The destruction of demons and pigs was by no means the end of the story. *"Those tending the pigs ran off and reported this whole event in the city and countryside"* (Mk 5:14). By city (polis) only Hippos could have been meant and the countryside was the surrounding villages of the Hippene. In the Palestinian Talmud and by Origen (PG 14,270) one finds evidence of an old Jewish tradition. It says that this region was inhabited by the Girgashites who had been driven away from

Eretz Israel by Joshua's conquest. They had belonged to the seven indigenous peoples of the country, of whom we read in Joshua 3:10: *"This is how you will know that the living God is among you and that he will certainly drive out before you the Canaanites, Hittites, Hivites, Perizzites, Girgashites, Amorites and Jebusites."*

Perhaps the original text of Mark, which has caused so much confusion, namely, *"They went across the lake to the region of the Gerasenes,"* should have read simply "They went across the lake to the country of expelled people" (Hebrew: Gerushim or Gerashim). Perhaps Origen quite rightly surmised a prophetic intent behind this designation. The moment the hellenized Girgashites or Gerasenes (i.e., the injured party as regards the pigs) discovered that the exorcist was an intruder from Israel and that he was responsible for the loss of the herd, they implored him to leave their region. The expelled became the expellers.

Jesus, who had conquered the storm on the lake and driven out the demons, yielded to the free will of human beings. His first attempt at bringing the message of salvation into heathen territory had failed.

But not completely. The man who had been tortured by the demons begged to go with him (Mk 5:18). However, out of consideration for the apostles and the sensitivity of his countrymen, Jesus was unable to take him along. Still, Jesus responded to the good will of this man in a different way. In all other cases of healing Jesus repeatedly admonished the cured person to tell no one what had happened. But in this particular case he explicitly instructs him: *"Go home to your family and tell them how much the Lord has done for you, and how he has had mercy on you"* (Mk 5:19). Jesus himself was barred from coming into this region, and so he commissioned this grateful and devoted man to spread the Good News. A splendid sentence concludes this episode of violent conflict between the Kingdom of God and that of Satan: *"So the man went away and began to tell in the Decapolis how much Jesus had done for him. And all the people were amazed"* (Mk 5:20).

In the boat again with his disciples on the way back to his own town (cf Mt 9:19) Jesus could have looked back towards the massive mountain ridge of the Hippene, and somehow the rocky cliffs of that

The basilica of Kursi

Greek ›City on the Mountain‹ may have appeared less hostile and menacing. In less than four centuries a magnificent cathedral would stand there on those heights. The presence of a bishop of Hippos at the very first Church Councils (Nicea, Constantinople, etc.) will bear witness of how Christianity conquered heathendom. Did the Christians of Hippos remember their first missionary by building the chapel which can still be seen at the site of his tomb-cave on the slope above Kursi?

6. ON THE WAY BACK HOME

After the stirring events in the country of the Gerasenes the untroubled crossing of the lake brought calm to the group of disciples around Jesus. As the boats landed close to the bay which had been the scene of the off-shore sermon the previous day, Jesus was met by excited crowds from Capernaum. One of the synagogue heads named Jairus pushed his way through the crowds to Jesus and called: *"'My little daughter is dying. Please come and put your hands on her so that she will be healed and live.' So Jesus went with him"* (Mk 5:23).

But soon there is another interruption: *"A large crowd followed and pressed around him. And a woman was there who had been subject to bleeding for twelve years. She had suffered a great deal under the care of many doctors and had spent all she had, yet instead of getting better she grew worse. When she heard about Jesus, she came up behind him in the crowd and touched his cloak"* (Mk 5:24-27).

Judging from what the great Church historian Eusebius (265-340) had to say about this woman, her conduct becomes more intelligible. According to him, she lived in Caesarea Philippi (Paneas). Eusebius had himself seen her house during a visit there. On a pillar at the entrance of her house stood a bronze statue of a kneeling woman stretching out her arms imploringly towards a young man. The bronze figure in all probability represented her own healing by Jesus (Hist. Eccl. VII, 18). The making of such a statue was only conceivable in a pagan-Christian milieu. If this tradition is valid, a lot becomes clear. She must have been a pagan woman of some means. When the news of the miracle worker of Capernaum reached her in Caesarea Philippi, she decided to go down and look for him. She knew the importance of ritual cleanliness to Jews. In Jewish eyes she must have appeared doubly unclean: first as a pagan and then because of her suffering from flow of blood (hemorrhage).

She stole up to Jesus secretly through the crowds, *"If I just touch his clothes, I will be healed"* (Mk 5:28). And indeed she was healed. Delirious with joy she meant to sneak away when her ears caught the voice of the man asking, *"Who touched my clothes?"* Feeling Jesus' searching look, the woman, knowing what had happened to her, came and fell at his feet and, trembling with fear, told him the whole truth. He said to her, *"Daughter, your faith has healed you. Go in peace and be freed from your suffering"* (Mk 5:33-34). Jesus did not want her to return home loaded with oppressive feelings of guilt, as though she had "stolen" her healing.

47

Late Byzantine reports speak of a stone in the form of a cross (Petra Haemorrhoissae) which designated the site where the healing took place. It was about a mile away from Capernaum and Heptapegon, the Seven Springs. As the original commemorative stone is not to be found, another stone has been erected on the approximate spot, enabling modern-day pilgrims to reflect on the biblical scene.

Jesus' first and eventful journey into pagan country ended with the raising of the twelve-year-old daughter of Jairus in his house in Capernaum. The attentive and sober words of Jesus, telling the people to give her something to eat (Mk 5:43b) breaks the tension of this dramatic chain of events and brings people back to the reality of everyday life.

JESUS
AND HIS
BROTHERS

Two groups felt themselves particularly close to Jesus: first, his immediate family circle and second, the Group of Twelve, his spiritual family. A passage at the beginning of the Gospel according to John and one at the beginning of the Acts of the Apostles reveal to us that there were moments when both families co-existed harmoniously. John writes: *"After this* (the wedding at Cana) *he went down to Capernaum with his mother and brothers and his disciples. There they stayed for a few days"* (Jn 2:12). Acts 1:14 states after the ascension of Jesus into heaven: *"They all joined together constantly in prayer, along with the women and Mary the mother of Jesus, and with his brothers."*

1. JESUS WITH HIS RELATIVES IN NAZARETH

However, between the wedding at Cana and the praying together in preparation for Pentecost, the two groups moved away from each other and there were times of great tension. To the relatives in Nazareth who certainly loved Jesus dearly, it appeared as though they had lost their son and brother to the new group of the Twelve. The people of the Nazarene clan who wanted to retrieve Jesus by force and who dismissed him with the words: *"He is out of his mind"* (Mk 3:21), must have influenced Jesus' immediate family: "Try to bring your son and brother to his right mind!"

When Jesus' brothers and sisters arrived together with his mother at Peter's house and called for Jesus, they must have experienced a painful sense of rejection at Jesus' response. He made it perfectly clear that his relationship to his disciples was of a far more fundamental nature and of more importance to his mission than connections to his family and relatives: *"'Who are my mother and my brothers?' he asked. Then he looked at those seated in a circle around him and said, 'Here are my mother and my brothers! Whoever does God's will is my brother and sister and mother.'"* (Mk 3:33-35). Like most families, this family also had to learn slowly that the time for letting go, the time to allow him the freedom to seek and to go his own way, had come.

Jesus' own experience when visiting Nazareth may have contributed much to the divergence of the two groups. Mark tells us of a visit which Jesus paid to his native town after his first journey into pagan territory (cf. Mk 6:1-6). The report by Luke, who apparently had access to sources from within the family circle, is somewhat longer (Lk 4:16-30). As both reports are important for the further development of Jesus' life, it is necessary to take a closer look.

In the pericope of Mark people ask themselves where Jesus got his wisdom, which he had evidently acquired: *"Isn't this the carpenter? Isn't this Mary's son and the brother of James, Joseph, Judas and Simon? Aren't his sisters here with us?"* (Mk 6:3). In an even older text than that of St Mark, namely that of St Paul writing to the Galatians, we find that he also names James as the Lord's brother (Ga 1:19).

The question of the degree of the kinship between Jesus and his brothers and sisters receives various answers in the traditions of the Eastern and Western Churches. In the Protestant Churches it is generally considered that they were Jesus' own younger brothers and sisters. The Catholic Church favors the opinion of Jerome that they were in fact his cousins. In the East it is customary to regard all extended family relations as brothers and sisters. The oldest interpretation, which is to be found with the Early Fathers, still lives on in the Oriental Churches, including the Greek Orthodox. According to this tradition Joseph was a widower when he took Mary to be his wife. His first wife bore him four sons and two daughters. Mary had only one son of her own but raised all of them and was greatly esteemed by all as their mother. This interpretation goes back to the Protevangelium of James, written in the second century. It certainly contains many additions. But its ascription to James ›the Lord's brother‹ allows one to assume that it also contains authentic family records. The tradition that the ›Brothers‹ of the Lord mean half-brothers may belong to such a category.

I disagree that it was only belief in the Virgin Birth that gave rise to this tradition, as it is often claimed. The discovery of the Scrolls of Qumran has given new access to and a better understanding of the events that could have led up to the birth of Jesus. According to the oldest sources the words of Mary to the angel at the Annunciation *"How will this be, since I do not know man?"* (Lk 1:34), are interpreted to mean that Mary felt herself bound by a vow of continence (chastity). Experts on present-day rabbinical Judaism and the pharisaical Judaism of the Second Temple period maintain that such a behavior could not be Jewish. In the Pharisaic view the very first duty of a person is to marry and to have children to ensure the continuation of a family line.

But today we know that Jews who were influenced by the Essene school thought differently. In the Temple Scroll, which was found in one of the Qumran caves, opened after the Six-Day War and published by Y. Yadin, the following instructions were found: "If a girl takes such a vow of continence without her father knowing about it, the father then is entitled to nullify it. Otherwise both are bound to

Part of the Temple scroll (with kind permission from the Israel Museum - Shrine of the Book)

keep it. Should a married woman take such a vow without her husband knowing about it, he can declare such a vow void. Should he, however, agree to such a step, both are bound to keep it (cf 11Q 53,16-20; 54,1-3).

Could not both possibilities apply to Mary? Mary's father then could have entrusted her to a man, who was prepared to acknowledge such a vow. Seeing that the widowed Joseph (of Davidic line) already had children, he could have found it easier to agree. The family Haggadah of the Protevangelium sees it essentially like this, even though many details in it may be sheer fantasy.

So the great astonishment of Joseph, who was regarded by his neighbourhood as a Tzaddik, a righteous man (›dikaios on‹ Mt 1,19), also becomes understandable. In the Jewish community a Tzaddik is a faithful observer of the Law. Was not his oldest son James the leader (bishop) of the first messianic community of Jews in Jerusalem, who carried the name Tzaddik (Jakobus ho dikaios) - James the Just? This is surely a title that both could have earned by their conscientious observance of the Torah.

The carpenter Joseph (*"Isn't this the carpenter's son? Isn't his mother's name Mary, aren't his brothers James, Joseph, Simon and Judas?"* Mt 13:55) and the carpenter Jesus (*"Isn't this the carpenter? Isn't this Mary's son and the brother of James, Joseph, Judas and Simon? Aren't his sisters here with us?"* Mk 6:3) remind us of a story told in the Talmud. A man arrives in a town, looking for someone who can solve a problem. He asks the people whether a rabbi lives there. On receiving a negative reply, he asks: "Is there a carpenter among you, the son of a carpenter,

52

who can offer me a solution?" (cf. Jacob Levy, Wörterbuch über Talmudim und Midraschim, Berlin, 1924, III, p. 338). This seems to indicate that the carpenter in a hamlet like Nazareth was the best qualified person for questions concerning the Halakhah. While plying their trade Joseph the Tzaddik and Jesus the Tzaddik might in all probability have been such people.

2. IN THE SYNAGOGUE IN NAZARETH

So it is not in the least surprising that Jesus went to the synagogue on the Shabbath and taught there. The fact that the Natzoreans, instead of using the synagogue of nearby Japhia, had their own synagogue in spite of the smallness of the village, may indicate that they followed a Halakhah that differed from that of their neighbors. The expression that Mark uses for Jesus' listeners, *"the many* (hoi polloi) *who heard him"* (Mk 6:2), is identical to that used by the Essene Qumran sources when referring to the members of their community: ›Ha Rabim‹, the Many.

From the Jewish writer, Philo of Alexandria, we have a description of the Essenes' way of life and their customs. The Essenes lived in various Jewish cities and towns, mostly in self-contained settlements. About their observance of the Shabbath, he writes: "They regard the seventh day as holy. On that day they abstain from work and go to sacred places that they call synagogues. They seat themselves according to their age in specific places, the younger ones below the elder, ready to listen attentively. Then one of them takes the scroll and reads from it, another more experienced person comes forward and explains what is not easy to understand. The greater part of their Teaching of Wisdom consists in an interpretation of symbols according to old and proven methods" (Quod omnis probus liber sit, 81-82).

The feeling that such or similar customs were observed in the synagogue in Nazareth is confirmed when we read the Lucan text (Lk 4:16-30).

The turn-about from initial enthusiasm to the utter rejection of Jesus at this assembly of Natzoreans is so sudden that the exegetes quite rightly think that this account is a compilation of several visits Jesus paid to Nazareth. It is assumed that in the beginning his kin received him joyfully with proud enthusiasm; later on they raised questions; finally they utterly rejected him, culminating in an attempt on his life.

The synagogue service that Jesus attended on that particular Shabbath comprised as usual prayers and two readings, one from the Torah and the other from the Prophets, the so-called Haphtarah. Then followed, if necessary, a translation into Aramaic (Targum) and the sermon.

"As he stood up to read, the scroll of the prophet Isaiah was handed to him" (Lk 4:16-17). The Haphtarah which Jesus read was certainly much longer than the short pericope (Lk 4:18-19) Luke quotes. Luke may well have drawn from the memories of the Jesus-family (at the time of Simon Bar-Cleophas, a cousin and second Bishop of Jerusalem), so the quotation, although shortened, could be essentially historical. If we add to the quotation in Luke (Lk 4:18-19) the two preceding verses and add one verse, we have a text which must have been of singular relevance to the members of the Natzorean clan. In this way it may be possible to find the psychological causes which brought about such a complete reversal of attitude towards Jesus.

Let us have a look at the Isaiah-text with this in mind:

A typical contemporary mosaic motif

60, 20b *...the Lord will be your everlasting light,*
       and your days of sorrow will end.
   21 *Then will all your people be righteous (Tzadikim)*
       and they will possess the land for ever.
       They are the shoot (netzer) that I have planted,
       the work of my hands,
       for the display of my splendor.
   22 *The least of you will become a thousand,*
       the smallest a mighty nation.
       I am the Lord;
       in its time I will do this swiftly.
61, 1 *The Spirit of the Sovereign Lord is on me,*
       because the Lord has anointed me
       to preach good news to the poor.
       He has sent me to bind up the broken-hearted,
       to proclaim freedom for the captives
       and release from darkness for the prisoners,
   2 *to proclaim the year of the Lord's favor*
       and the day of vengeance of our God,
       to comfort all who mourn,
   3 *and provide for those who grieve in Zion –*
       to bestow on them a crown of beauty instead of ashes,
       the oil of gladness
       instead of mourning,
       and a garment of praise
       instead of a spirit of despair.
       They will be called oaks of
       righteousness,
       a planting of the Lord
       for the display of his splendor.

This or something slightly longer could have been the passage from the Haphtarah (reading of the Prophets) which Jesus read out to his clan in the synagogue.

...and your days of sorrow will end.... (Evening at the Lake)

3. NAZARETH OR CAPERNAUM

Jesus must have known that in this passage from Isaiah lay the deeply-rooted hopes of his kinsmen. After reading the passage, he returned the scroll to the synagogue attendant and sat down. No wonder that the eyes of ›the many‹ were fastened onto him, as he started to speak: *"Today this scripture is fulfilled in your hearing"* (Lk 4:21).

It must have aroused the enthusiasm of his audience. For the author of Trito-Isaiah deals here with the eschatological restoration of Israel. Such words naturally carried a special force in the ears of Natzoreans. The words: *"the shoot* (netzer) *that I have planted"* were exactly tailored to them. The founder of the Qumran Essenes also reflected in his hymns (psalms) on these words and applied them to his community (1QH 6,15; 7,19; 7,6,8,10).

But all the more did they fit the Davidic clan. The shoot from the stump of Jesse (cf Isaiah 11:1) was still present and alive in the hearts of the Natzoreans. Zerubbabel of Davidic descent (cf. 1Chr 3:17-19)had become governor of Judea but after the commencement of rebuilding the Temple (December 521 B.C., according to Haggai 2:18) he disappeared from the annals of history.*"The hands of Zerubbabel have laid the foundation of this temple"* (Zech 4:9). After that the Davidic clan also disappeared into the mist of the Babylonian Diaspora. Although impoverished and dispersed the bold hope remained ever alive in their consciousness that the Messiah would come from out of their midst. They were the ›faithful remnant‹ of Israel, through whom the light of God's glory would shine. *"The least of you will become a thousand, the smallest a mighty nation"* (Is 60:22a). The Lord will bring it about *"in its time"* (Is 60:22b).

Was this the moment?

And could this man from their own clan, the son of Joseph, of whom they had already heard such marvellous things, become their leader? Perhaps through him honor might be bestowed upon them as well. *"All spoke well of him and were amazed at the gracious words that came from his lips"* (Lk 4:22).

But soon came disenchantment. The son of Joseph had his own plans. Why was he working down in Capernaum among those simple-minded fishermen? Wasn't Nazareth his home town where he should display his miraculous powers? *"Physician, heal yourself!"* (Lk 4:23) Jesus points out from Israel's history that God acts differently: Elijah was sent to a widow in Zarephath in the region of Sidon, not to a widow in Israel. Likewise Elisha cleansed the foreigner Naaman the Syrian and not a leper of his own country.

The Natzoreans were bitterly disappointed. They believed that Jesus' kinship with their clan gave them legitimate claims on his person. Now they found earlier fears confirmed. Then elders of Jesus' clan had sent a delegation to Capernaum. Mark tells us about this: *"Again a crowd gathered, so that Jesus and his disciples were not even able to eat. When his people heard of this, they went out to lay hold of him; for they said: 'He is out of his mind'"* (Mk 3:20-21).

Tidings of what was happening in Capernaum had leaked to Nazareth and seemed alarming. The elders had learned that this man from their own ranks was so much sought after by enthusiastic crowds that he hardly found time to eat. They felt a responsibility towards this promising young prophet. A delegation of his *own people* was sent to bring him back to Nazareth. He should not burn himself out too soon. They were instructed that in case he did not return voluntarily, they should exercise the rights of kinship and bring him back if necessary by force (Mk 3:21). When they failed in their mission to draw Jesus out of his immediate circle of the Twelve disciples and the enthusiastic crowds, they returned and reported disparagingly, *"He is out of his mind."*

Now that Jesus had once more visited them, they found that what they had feared was confirmed. "Nothing can be done for him: he is mad". Jesus did not want to put himself at the service of the high-flown ambitions of his countrymen and their hopes for the future. For centuries the clan of Natzoreans had been conscious of their own divine election and had, especially under the influence of Essenes, become absorbed with themselves. Jesus knew that such restriction would jeopardize his whole mission: *"'I tell you the truth,' he continued, 'no prophet is accepted in his home town'"* (Lk 4:24).

His tribesmen were furious. It came to an open breach. They drove him through the streets and would have thrown him down a cliff, *"but he walked right through the crowd and went on his way"* (Lk 4:30), *"down to Capernaum"* (Lk 4:31).

Relief from the synagogue in Capernaum, that was built at the end of the 4th cent. above the one where Jesus prayed

4. JESUS AND HIS BROTHERS GO THEIR OWN WAYS

After the breach in Nazareth we hear nothing precise about what happened to the members of Jesus' family. Did they have to leave Nazareth as well? It seems as though they still wanted to be near to him. According to one tradition they eventually belonged to the group of the Seventy (Lk 10:1-17).

However, for the time being tension between the group of Twelve and Jesus' brothers continued. John reports a revealing incident (Jn 7:2-12)

"But when the Jewish Feast of Tabernacles was near, Jesus' brothers said to him, 'You ought to leave here and go to Judea, so that your disciples may see the miracles you do. No-one who wants to become a public figure acts in

secret. Since you are doing these things, show yourself to the world.' For even his own brothers did not believe in him" (Jn 7:2-5).

This passage mentions two facts:

1. In spite of many disappointments the brothers of Jesus persisted in their attempts to maintain links with the young charismatic from their family. They displayed a personal interest that the work of their brother should become known to a wider public even if, understandably, there was also the hope that something of his fame would reflect upon them as well.

2. However, what strikes one particularly is that they were well aware that Jesus also had disciples in Judea, and cherished the desire that he should not neglect those living in the important area of Jerusalem's sphere of influence. What disciples did the brothers of Jesus have in mind?

They may well have been isolated family members from Bethany near Jerusalem or disciples from Emmaus. In my opinion they could possibly have been sympathizers on Mount Zion in Jerusalem, the place which later formed the center of the early Christian community. Recent research and the discovery of the Gate of the Essenes has shown that it was also the location of an Essene "monastery" with a community attached to it.

John reports that Jesus had driven the traders from the Temple in the days before the Jewish Passover of the previous year. This courageous act had attracted many people's attention to Jesus. They *"saw the miraculous signs he was doing and believed in his name"* (Jn 2:23).

It can hardly be doubted that the cleansing of the Temple would have had a strong impact precisely on Essene circles, which comprised many priests. Their principal charge against the Sadducean Temple priests was precisely that the Temple had been polluted. Although they still visited the Temple because it was God's dwelling, they strictly refused to offer sacrifice there. In particular they criticized the Hasmonean high priests for the introduction of certain holy days which according to their opinion were no longer biblical, but based on Babylonian-Persian calendar models. The circles of Essenes used a solar calender of 364 days (precisely 52 weeks), so that the Feast of the Passover fell regularly on the third Wednesday of the first month. Sukkoth, the Feast of Tabernacles, also took place regularly on a Wednesday among the Essene circles, whereas it was a moveable feast for the Pharisees and also in the Temple observance.

Jesus' cleansing of the Temple won him the enthusiastic acclaim of many Jewish circles. This enthusiasm however did not find the expected echo within Jesus himself. *"But Jesus would not entrust himself to them for he knew all men. He did not need man's testimony about man, for he knew what was in a man"* (Jn 2:24-25). The phrase "for he knew all men" does not necessarily reflect supernatural knowledge, but could simply imply that he had had contacts with these Essenic groups when visiting Jerusalem on earlier pilgrimages in the company of his brothers. However, no firm or considered deliberate connections were further developed.

Did his brothers become the mouth-piece for these ›disciples‹, urging Jesus to take a little more notice of them? With sharp insight Jesus realized that the question of faith in his Person was the deepest problem in his preaching of the Good News. He was looking for discipleship, not admiration. His brothers wanted to show him the way, not follow him. In this sense "they did not believe in him."

From the earliest times exegetes have been rather embarrassed in their attempts to find an answer to why Jesus replied so evasively. For many scholars it presents an insoluble problem. In a determined reply to the brothers he informed them that he did not want to go to Jerusalem for Sukkoth, the Feast of Tabernacles. *"However, after his brothers had left for the Feast, he went also, not publicly, but in secret"* (Jn 7:10). The Feast attended by Jesus was celebrated in the Temple. To my mind the best solution to the whole discussion of this pericope is to assume that two different calendars are involved. From the discoveries at Qumran it is clear today that two different calendars were in use in the time of Jesus. Sadducees and Pharisees adhered to one calendar and the group related to the Essenes followed the other.

Jesus deliberately moved in the circles of Pharisees during his public activity in Capernaum and therefore at that time he also observed, together with his apostles, the normal calendar of the Temple. Therefore he could address his brothers:

"'The right time (kairos) *for me has not yet come; for you any time is right... You go to the Feast. I am not yet going up to this Feast, because for me the right time has not yet come.' Having said this, he stayed in Galilee"* (Jn 7:6-9). Jesus does not use the word ›hour‹ which refers in John to the hour of Jesus' death, but ›kairos‹ (the appropriate time) to indicate that the date for the Feast that Jesus was following had not yet arrived.

The word ›kairos‹ is also used in this sense in the Book of Daniel in a vision that may have been alluding to Antiochus Epiphanes (175-163 B.C.), who played a very destructive role in Jewish life. It speaks of the arrival of a fourth king, who will change the set times and the laws (Daniel 7:25). In the Septuagint the word "kairos" is also used for the festal seasons, i.e., for the calendars of Holy Days.

So the brothers of Jesus went to Jerusalem for Sukkoth on their own. This feast was not celebrated on the Temple compound but, as can be presumed, on the southwest hill of the city, not far from the Gate of the Essenes (Josephus Flavius, B.J. 5,145) where the solar calendar of the Book of Jubilees prevailed. According to this calendar the various feasts were generally celebrated before those of the Temple.

When the usual time for the Feast of Tabernacles (Sukkoth) approached, Jesus too went with his apostles to Jerusalem. He celebrated the Feast together with the people in the Temple and taught there. *"Not until halfway through the Feast did Jesus go up to the temple courts and begin to teach"* (Jn 7:14).

On the last day of the Feast of Tabernacles it was the custom to bring water from Siloam's Pool in a festive ceremonial procession to the Temple and pour it over the altar of burnt offerings. At this moment *"on the last and greatest day of the Feast, Jesus stood and cried in a*

loud voice, 'If anyone is thirsty, let him come to me and drink. Whoever be-
lieves in me, as the Scripture has said, streams of living water will flow from
within him'" (Jn 7:37-38).

5. THE RECONCILIATION

Jesus himself must have suffered from the tension between his two
rival families, each wishing to be close to him. According to a short
quotation from the lost Jewish-Christian ›Gospel According to the
Hebrews‹ (›Gospel of the Nazarenes‹ as it is called by modern scholars), the Lord's brother James, who certainly did not belong to the
Twelve, managed somehow to participate in the last Passover celebrated by Jesus. To my mind this took place in the Essene guesthouse
on Mount Zion on the Tuesday night. Still the uncomfortable tension
between Jesus' family and the Twelve persisted.

The great reconciliation took place as Jesus was hanging on the
cross. Looking down he saw two persons, who were very dear to him.
They were symbolical representatives of the two rival groups: his
mother and the beloved disciple (John). He begged them to accept
each other: *"He said to his mother, 'Woman, behold your son,' then he said*
to his disciple, 'Here is your mother.' From that time on, this disciple took
her into his home" (Jn 19:26b-27). From the cross where he wanted "to
draw everything to himself" he united his two families. The reconciliation was one of the fruits of his sacrificial death. Tradition has it that
Mary lived in Jerusalem on Mt .Zion, where John lived together with
the members of her Natzorean family.

We see the two groups reconciled and united in the ›upper room‹
after Jesus' Resurrection and Ascension: the Eleven were there *"along*
with the women and Mary the mother of Jesus, and with his brothers" (Acts
1:14). Together they awaited the outpouring of the Spirit; together
they experienced the birth of the Church. Both groups, the Twelve as
well as Jesus' natural family, were constitutive elements of the
Church of Christ. Simon headed the Twelve. James, the Lord's

From the first epistle of **Paul to the Corinthians**:

"For what I received I passed on to you
as of first importance:
that Christ died for our sins
according to the Scriptures,
that he was buried,
that he was raised on the third day
according to the Scriptures,
and that he appeared to **Kephas** (Peter), and then to the Twelve.
...Then he appeared to **James,**
then to all the apostles..."

(1 Cor 15:3-7).

Paul mentions that the Lord's brother James as well as Peter had a personal apparition of Jesus. From an apocryphal gospel that has been lost one citation was preserved as reported by Jerome.

Jerome writes in ›De Viris Illustribus‹:
"The Gospel which is called ›According to the Hebrews‹ and which I recently translated into Greek and Latin... reports after the Resurrection of the Lord:
...When the Lord had handed over the linen cloth to the priest's servant, he went to James and appeared to him. For James had made an oath to eat no bread after he had drunk the cup of the Lord until he saw him risen from those who sleep.
Shortly thereafter the Lord said to him: *bring a table here with bread.* Straightway it adds: *he took the bread, spoke the blessing and gave it to James the Just and said to him: "My brother, eat your bread, for the Son of Man is risen from those who are asleep"* (PL 23, 642-643).

brother, headed Jesus' family. Both groups had journeyed a long way to faith, which only came to maturity in Christ's Resurrection. According to the oldest account of the Resurrection as transmitted by Paul (1 Cor 15:1-17) the Lord had appeared personally to both Peter and James, as the leaders responsible for the two groups. Both were reputed to be pillars (Ga 2:9) of the Church.

The one became the head of the universal Church, the other the head of the Church of the Jews in the Holy Land.

ECCLESIA EX
GENTILITATE

ECCLESIA EX
CIRCUMCISIONE

JESUS' SECOND GALILEAN JOURNEY: FROM THE FIRST TO THE SECOND FEEDING OF THE MULTITUDE

1. THE DEATH OF THE BAPTIST

It was probably in the spring of the year 29 A.D. that the disturbing news reached Capernaum of the execution of John the Baptist and also that Jesus himself was suspected by the "King" of being a second John (cf. Mk 6:16).

While the synoptic Gospels see the reason for the Baptist's death in the hatred of Herodias, the unlawful wife of Herod Antipas, the historian Flavius Josephus gives us to believe that the principal motive behind the removal of the Baptist was political. The dance of Herodias' daughter in the fortress of Machaerus may well have been the triggering factor. We can better appreciate why the danger facing Jesus was rooted in the suspicion of Herod the tetrarch when we read the report of Josephus:

"Herod (Antipas) had had [John the Baptist] executed, although he was a good man, who urged the Jews to practice virtue, both in righteousness towards one another and in piety towards God, and so to come to be baptized... Very many people flocked together when they heard this message and Herod feared that the regard in which the man was held could lead his people to rebellion. For his advice was generally followed in everything. He thought it was therefore better for him to take the initiative and clear him out of the way before he was in a position to incite a popular rebellion, than to wait for unrest and be unable to restore the situation in which he would be involved. On the grounds of this suspicion Herod had John put in chains and brought to the fortress of Machaerus and executed there" (Ant 18, 116-119).

The beheading of John and the superstitious suspicions of Herod Antipas that Jesus was the Baptist returned from the dead and was continuing his work, meant that at the whim of the tyrant in the fortress of Tiberias Jesus might suffer the same fate of John. For now around Jesus, who had been working for over a year in Galilee, great crowds of people gathered as they once did around John. It was easy for people to suspect that Jesus and his disciples were close to the Zealots of Gamla and were secretly forging revolutionary plans together. The ›Fox of Tiberias‹ (cf. Lk 13:31) might decide it was better

The threat from *the tyrant in the fortress of Tiberias* (View from the Eremos cave)

to deal quickly with this popular prophet from Capernaum before it was too late. It can be ascertained that from this moment on Jesus avoided whatever might give the ruler of Galilee ground to throw him into prison. For this reason he avoided crowds and never remained long in one place.

2. THE FIRST MIRACLE OF FEEDING (MK 6:30-44)

Mark tells us that after the debacle in Nazareth Jesus had sent his twelve disciples in pairs to bring the good news into the Galilean villages (Mk 6:7). Their work was, in the first place, to bring the good tidings to their own people. The Gentiles and the Samaritans were excluded (cf. Mt 10:5). The disciples *"went out and preached that people should repent. They drove out many demons and anointed many sick people with oil and healed them"*(Mk 6:12-13).

On their return to Capernaum from their missionary work great numbers of people began to flock there wanting to see the master with their own eyes. The coming and going of such large numbers brought fresh danger, not just because Jesus and his disciples *"did not even have a chance to eat"* (Mk 6:31), but also because Herod's suspicion would find new nourishment.

Then Jesus said to his disciples: *"'Come with me by yourselves to a quiet place and get some rest.' So they went away by themselves by boat to a solitary place to be alone"* (Mk 6:31-32). The people who had gathered from the various towns must have been disappointed when they saw their Rabbi Jesus leaving with his disciples. However, when they saw that the boat suddenly turned in towards the nearby Seven Springs (Ma-gadan, present day Tabgha) they ran the two miles along the shore, never losing sight of the boat and *"got there ahead of them"* (Mk 6:33). Anyone who knows the area around the lake must realize that this last statement of Mark completely excludes the possibility held by most commentators who accept only one feeding, and that the boat landed on the other side of the lake. The distance would have

...in springtime, when the Jordan is very high....(North of Bethsaida)

been 15 - 20 miles and it is unthinkable that in springtime, when the Jordan is very high, this large jostling crowd of people could have crossed over so quickly as to have reached there before the boat arrived. Therefore I believe the old Jewish-Christian tradition which Egeria picked up (see box p. 36) to be well founded in that it indicates present-day Tabgha as the place of the first feeding.

When Jesus saw the crowd, whom he had tried to avoid, he could easily have sailed somewhere else, but his heart got the better of him. He got out of the boat, *"for he had compassion on them, because they were like sheep without a shepherd. So he began teaching them many things"* (Mk 6:34). Too many for his disciples it seems, who asked one another what they were to do with this huge crowd of people who had gathered there on the spur of the moment without bringing food with them. As evening drew near, they no doubt thought that, though Jesus needed so little himself, he must have forgotten that these people must now be hungry.

They said to him: *"This is a remote place, and it's already very late. Send the people away so that they can go to the surrounding countryside and villages and buy themselves something to eat"* (Mk 6:35-36). It really would not have been a problem. Even if there was nothing in the uninhabited Ma-gadan (Tabgha) other than perhaps an isolated mill, the village of Gennesaret was only a few thousand feet beyond Tel Kinneret; the village of Khor rested a little higher up the hillside and it

...grass grows abundantly in springtime ... Among the Tabgha springs, in front of the ›Bath of the Leper‹

was not far to Capernaum and Korazin. The apostles must have been taken aback when Jesus told them *"You give them something to eat."* He wanted to indicate "These are our guests. Where is your hospitality?" Or perhaps, as John says, he simply wanted to test them: *"He asked this only to test them, for he already had in mind what he was going to do"* (Jn 6:6).

This first feeding at the Heptapegon was a free gift of his kindness, not the result of necessity. Following the rather confused thoughts of the disciples about buying bread and paying for it, Jesus asked: *"How many loaves do you have? Go and see"* (Mk 6:38). Five loaves and two fish, probably of the kind dried in the sun, were brought. Perhaps they belonged to a boy who was ready to share them with everybody (cf. Jn 6:9). Today as then, grass grows abundantly in springtime around the many rivulets and bizarre rock-formations, a product of the mineral waters. The people sat down on the grass in groups of hundreds and fifties just as their forefathers were used to doing on their journey through the Sinai desert (cf Ex 18:25).

The old Jewish-Christian tradition of Tabgha recounts that the Lord placed the five loaves and two fish on a large piece of rock which is visible today beneath the altar of the Church of the Multiplication. *"Taking the five loaves and the two fish and looking up to heaven, he gave thanks* (Berakhah - the Jewish blessing) *and broke the loaves. Then he*

71

gave them to his disciples to set before the people. He also divided the two fish among them all. They all ate and were satisfied, and the disciples picked up twelve baskets full of broken pieces of bread and fish that remained" (Mk 6:4-43).

Everything in this report: the site, the placing of the groups and in particular the number of the twelve baskets (›kophinoi‹ are baskets without handles) points towards the fact that this feeding was meant for the twelve tribes of Israel.

Mosaic floor in the basilica in Tabgha with the historic rock

3. A STORMY NIGHT

The following report (Mk 6:45-54), which fits so exactly into this landscape where I have now lived for over 12 years, touches me each time I read it. *"Immediately Jesus made his disciples get into the boat and go on ahead of him to the other side of the lake to Bethsaida."* What had happened? Why the hurry? John knew the reason: *"After the people saw the miraculous sign that Jesus did, they began to say, 'Surely this is the prophet who is to come into the world.' Jesus, knowing that they intended to come and make him king by force, withdrew to a mountain by himself"* (Jn 6:14-15). This messianic upsurge was exactly what he wished to avoid. Herod, who in his palace in Tiberias lived within sight of the place of the feeding, certainly had spies among the crowd. The messianic enthusiasm of the masses was palpable, perhaps evoked by the imprudent talk of some of the disciples. He had to get his disciples into safety: "Get yourselves into the boats at once! Here we are in danger. Sail to the other side of the Jordan to the tetrarchy of Philip to Bethsaida. There wait for me!" He did not worry about his own safety: *"He dismissed the crowd. After leaving them, he went up the mountainside to pray"* (Mk 6:45b-46).

›The mountain‹ where he preferred to stay time and again rose above the springs of Ma-gadan. At the southern end, facing the lake, there is a grotto below a hanging cliff (known as the Eremos cave or Magharat Ayub) where Jesus could find shelter during his night

The Eremos cave

prayers. That particular night a cold east wind suddenly sprang up, the Sharkiyeh, dreaded by the fishermen. At the end of winter it can become particularly severe, endangering people on the lake. It becomes impossible to sail or row against that wind. Jesus was worried about his disciples whom he had sent on to Bethsaida and from which direction this violent Sharkiyeh blew. *"When evening came, the boat was in the middle of the lake, and he was alone on land. He saw the disciples straining at the oars, because the wind was against them"* (Mk 6:47-48). Finally he could watch no longer. He must go and help them. Without much ado he hurried down to the lake. *"About the fourth watch of the night he went out to them, walking on the lake... when they saw him walking on the lake, they thought he was a ghost. They cried out, because they all saw him and were terrified. Immediately he spoke to them and said, 'Take courage! It is I. Don't be afraid'"* (Mk 6: 48b-50).

Matthew inserts here the scene with Peter (Mt 14:28-31), who tried to cross the waves towards Jesus: *"But when he saw the wind, he was afraid and, beginning to sink, cried out, 'Lord, save me!'"* (Mt 14:30). Jesus, having stretched out his hand to save him, climbed into the boat together with Peter. Jesus must have noticed how exhausted his disciples were after their long and useless rowing against wind and waves. In the meantime the wind had dropped and he told them not to continue the lengthy journey to Bethsaida but to take the shortest course to the shore. So they went ashore at Gennesaret (cf. Mk 6:53; Mt 14:34).

4. FROM GENNESARET TO PHOENICIA

To the west of Tabgha lies a hill (Tel Kinnerot) which can be seen from a distance. Today its hollowed out interior contains the huge pumping station that takes water out of the lake and distributes it throughout Israel. Once, the chief town of the tribe of Naphtali, Kinneret or Kinnerot, was situated on the top of this hill. Further west lies the fertile plain of Ginnosar. The recent excavations carried out on

Tel Kinneret have proved that this Israelite stronghold was destroyed during the campaign of Tiglat-Pileser III in the year 732 BC. There were later attempts by the Assyrians and the Persians to settle there but around 200 BC the hill was abandoned. In Hellenistic times a new settlement was started at the foot of the Tel, near the so-called ›Fig Spring‹. Its name was hellenized to ›Gennesaret‹.

Jesus now landed there with his disciples. In spite of a sleepless night they could find no rest. *"As soon as they got out of the boat, people recognized Jesus. They ran throughout that whole region and carried the sick on mats wherever they heard he was"* (Mk 6:54-55). One gets the impression that Jesus was in a hurry to leave Galilee which was no longer safe for him. Even though the messianic enthusiasm of the previous day had come to nothing, too long a stay in one place could arouse the suspicion of Herod. Mark mentions the small group walking swiftly through villages, cities and farms (Mk 6:56) until they reached the border of Phoenicia.

Jesus' intention was apparently to get out of the danger zone of Galilee as soon as possible, in order to spend some quiet days with his apostles in Phoenicia. This is what he had intended to do in the Eremos of Tabgha–Ma-gadan, but had been unable to do. The shortest and fastest way from Gennesaret to the *"region of Tyre"* (Mk 7:24) led through Wadi Amud to Gischala. From there it was but a few miles to the Phoenician border. This route took them through one of the wildest and most beautiful nature areas of Galilee. Today a nature reserve, it remains almost untouched by human hand and offers some of the richest variety of flora and fauna of this blessed land.

We can imagine how this small group of disciples travelled along the edge of the fertile plain of Ginnosar and upon entering Wadi Amud passed the big cave that today is called ›Me'arat Golgolet‹ (Cave of the skull: some 1900 years later the petrified remains of Homo Galileensis, a 60,000 year old caveman, were found here). It was before Passover (cf. Jn 6:4). Spring was in full bloom: among the many wild flowers the red anemones and pink cyclamens dazzled the eye. Peter and his companions kept their eyes open; leopards roamed the area and could have been dangerous. Rockbadgers were sunning themselves in front of their holes. Disturbed wild boars ran grunting for shelter behind dense bushes.

After a few hundred yards the group of travelers stood in front of a natural pillar that pointed like a huge thumb towards the sky. This pillar (›amud‹) lends its name to the entire valley. Further on the group around Jesus walked along the foot of a towering cliff, the perfect nesting place for the many vultures that circled in the sky above the valley. Then the path began to mount. They passed the rocks of Akabaron. Some thirty years later Josephus Flavius would be fortifying this settlement, as well as Safed further uphill, right on a mountain top. Centuries later the Crusaders would rebuild Safed into a formidable fortress but loose it to the Muslims. In the 16th century many Jews exiled from Spain would settle and build it into a commercially and spiritually thriving town.

From the villages and hamlets where the fame of the miracle worker of Capernaum had spread people came with their sick and laid them on the roadside *"and besought him that they might touch the fringe of his garment, and as many as touched it were made well"* (Mk 6:56).

Jerome mentions twice the small town of Gischala in northern Galilee as the home of the parents of the apostle Paul.
1. De Viris Illustribus: *"Paul, formerly Saul, an apostle outside the Twelve, came from the tribe Benjamin and the Judean town Gischala. He was captured by the Romans and came with his parents to Tarsus in Cilicia"* (PL 23, 646).

2. Commentary on Philemon: *"It is reported that the parents of the apostle Paul came from the Judean region of Gischala. When the whole province was destroyed by the Romans and the Jews were dispersed over the world, they were taken off to Tarsus, while the young Paul followed his parents in their fate"* PL 23,645-6. (ibid. notes ad loc)

In 4 BC and AD 6 Zealot rebellions occurred in that area which were firmly suppressed by the Romans (cf. B.J. 2,69; Ant. 17,271; 288-289).

This leads me to think that Jesus, like many pious Jews, wore a garment with tassels called ›tzitzit‹ attached to its four corners, as prescribed in the Torah (Num 15:38; Deut 22:12). In popular belief such fringes were considered having the power of a talisman, especially when worn by holy men.

But Jesus did not only receive admiration on this journey, but also opposition. In one place in particular a bitter dispute developed with some of the Pharisees. When Mark enumerates the various places Jesus passed through, he speaks also of ›cities‹. As Gischala was the only city in northern Galilee, the place could well have been this town, which today has its name arabized into Jish.

We know from its later history that the influence of the Pharisees and the Zealots in Gischala was very strong. St Jerome seems to know that the parents of St Paul came from Gischala and following a revolt were brought as prisoners to Tarsus. Sold as slaves they must have become freedmen later and as such been given Roman citizenship.

Pharisees and teachers of the law from Jerusalem had come to this remote place, probably to instruct the people in the Tradition of the Elders. These ›guardians of tradition‹ were fast to notice that some disciples of this famous miracle worker did not take these teachings serious enough since they would not rinse their hands before eating - a ritual, that was part of the tradition.

At the time Mark wrote his Gospel, the question of clean or unclean food was uppermost in the mind of believers, who had come partly from Judaism, partly from paganism. Mark has Jesus take a position decidedly against too strict an interpretation of the food laws: *"Nothing entering from outside into a man can make him 'unclean'. Rather, it is what comes out of a man that makes him 'unclean'"* (Mk 7:15).

The evangelist here adds his own interpretation: *"In saying this, Jesus declared all foods 'clean'"* (Mk 7:19b). He probably added this remark on the abolishment of the Jewish "Kashrut Laws"(laws on forbidden food) at this point because Jesus was planning to leave Galilee, in order to spend a longer period with his disciples among the Gentiles.

5. IN PHOENICIA: OPENING UP TO THE GENTILES

Mark tells us: *"Jesus left that place and went to the vicinity of Tyre"* (Mk 7:25). ("Tyre and Sidon" Mt 15:21). Here he was safe from possible interference by the unpredictable tetrarch Herod Antipas in Tiberias. Luke says that Herod had a desire to see Jesus (Lk 9:9) for the man, so he imagined, performed fine miracles. He had also *"liked to listen"* to John the Baptist (Mk 6:20b), whom he had later beheaded.

Now Jesus was in Phoenicia. This was a pagan region and he *"did not want anyone to know"* (Mk 7:24) of his presence there. This was not his field of action. He said emphatically: *"I was sent only to the lost sheep of Israel"* (Mt 15:24). He saw himself as a prophet sent to his own people. What made him change his mind was the distress of a mother and her pressing request. Suddenly she was there, this Syro-Phoenician mother.

Her daughter was ill, tormented by some evil spirit, she thought. She called out: *"Lord, Son of David, have mercy on me!"* (Mt 15:22) Jesus wanted to keep his resolution of not performing any miracles in gentile territory. The disciples tried to send the woman away. So Jesus went into a house. The woman slipped in as well. She fell to her knees in front of Jesus and begged *"Jesus to drive the demon out of her daughter. 'First let the children eat all they want,' he told her, 'for it is not right to take the children's bread and toss it to the dogs'"* (Mk 7:26b-27).

These words may well have been intended so that his disciples would understand his refusal. Down at Ma-gadan he had given his people bread after which twelve baskets full of leftovers had been collected, indicating that God's gift was ready for all the tribes of Israel. But neither the people nor his disciples had understood the deeper significance of what had happened; *"for they had not understood about the loaves; their hearts were hardened"* (Mk 6:52).

The pagan mother had also overheard what Jesus had said; indeed she had caught the rebuff he implied. Yet, she did not seem hurt. On the contrary she accepted the hard word but drew the consequence: *"'Yes, Lord,' she replied, 'but even the dogs under the table eat the crumbs from the children's table'"* (Mk 7:28). This was humble faith. Jesus was both surprised and deeply touched as he had often been whenever he noticed the faith of non-Jews. It had been the case with the centurion from Capernaum (Mt 8:10) and with the hemorrhaging woman from Caesarea Philippi (Mk 5:34). Jesus could not do otherwise but give up his opposition and answer: *"For the word you have spoken, you may go; you will find your daughter well"* (Mk 7:29). By healing from afar Jesus rewarded this pagan woman's faith.

The word of that pagan woman must have been reverberating in his mind."For the word you have spoken." What had she said? She had meant to say that not only the Jews needed him, but also the Gentiles. The Jews already had a covenant with the true God, while the Gentiles had none.

Neither Mark nor Matthew, who report Jesus' stay in the region of Tyre and Sidon, seem to have any idea what he did there or what happened within himself. What he did for this Syro-Phoenician woman must have made Jesus reflect: "Have I really been sent only to the lost sheep of the House of Israel? Does not this people need me far more?" Did, perhaps, his mother's words come to his mind, as he recalled Mary speaking of the prophesy of the devout old Simeon in the Temple (Lk 2:25), as he held him as a child in his arm? Mary may well have shared with her son the fruits of her pondering of these words in her heart (Lk 2:19). *"For my eyes have seen your salvation, which you have prepared in the sight of all people, light for the revelation to the Gentiles and for glory to your people Israel"* (Lk 2:30-32). Was he not a Natzorean, one of David's house? And what had the prophet Isaiah said in his Second Song of the Suffering Servant? *"It is too small a thing for you to be my servant to restore the tribes of Jacob and bring back the preserved of Israel (›natzorei Israel‹). I will also make you a light for the Gentiles, that you may bring my salvation to the ends of the earth"* (Isaiah 49:6).

6. IN THE DECAPOLIS AGAIN

As after the sermon by the lake, he again felt the urge to return to the heathen Decapolis. His first attempt had failed: he had not been accepted but he had sent the first missionary into that pagan land (Mk 4:20), the Gerasene who had been freed of the legion of demons. He wanted to go and see whether he might now find an atmosphere of acceptance.

...onto the Golan Heights...this is probably the way Jesus and his followers took....

"Then Jesus left the vicinity of Tyre and went through Sidon, down towards the Sea of Galilee and into the middle of the Decapolis" (Mk 7:31). It must have been a long walk. At that time a road led from the region of Tyre and Sidon through Caesarea Philippi onto the Golan Heights. It was the road over which grain was brought from Bosra to both these coastal towns (cf. Acts 12:20). This is probably the way Jesus and his followers took to reach the Hippene, the upland northern corner of the Decapolis. From here another route (still traceable today) led down to the lake situated 200 m. below sea level. They would have reached the shore near Tel Hadar.

As Jesus came this time over the Golan Heights into the Decapolis, he soon realized that he was no longer a stranger here, for the man he had healed at Kursi had praised him everywhere. Mark reports the healing of a deaf mute who had been brought to him (Mk 7:32-37). However, this would hardly have been the only healing if we are to believe the report of cumulative healings which we hear of in Matthew (Mt 15:30).

The people of Decapolis who had heard of the miraculous cure of the deaf-mute were enthusiastic. *"People were overwhelmed with amazement. 'He has done everything well,' they said. 'He even makes the deaf hear and the mute speak.'"* (Mk 7:37). We can assume that *"the big crowd which in those days (while Jesus was in the Decapolis) gathered around him"* (Mk 8:1) was made up to a large extent of Gentiles who followed him down to the hill (Tel Hadar) by the lake. They had even prepared themselves and brought provisions with them in baskets with handles (which we shall discuss later on) in order to be able to persevere with the Teacher for several days. But let Matthew tell us his version: *"Jesus left there and went along the Sea of Galilee. Then he went up on a hill (›oros‹) and sat down. Great crowds came to him, bringing the lame, the blind, the crippled, the mute and many others, and laid them at his feet; and he healed them. The people were amazed when they saw the mute speaking, the cripple made well, the lame walking and the blind seeing. And they praised the God of Israel"* (Mt 15: 29-31).

Matthew alludes to similar healings at the time John the Baptist sent his disciples to ask Jesus *"Are you the one who was to come, or should we expect someone else?"* (Mt 11:2) Jesus' reply then was, *"the blind receive sight, the lame walk, those who have leprosy are cured, the deaf hear"* (Mt 11:2-6). Now these signs of the dawning of the messianic era are repeated here among the Gentiles on the eastern shore. The people from the Decapolis were astounded. Not even their mightiest gods could perform anything like this. *"And they praised the God of Israel"*. For three days they remained with this prophet from Israel, eating of the provisions in their baskets which they had brought with them and drinking water from the lake. As it was now high summer they could easily spend the nights out in the open. Some of them may have fished for so-called ›Kinneret sardines‹ which one can still find in abundance today near the shore of Tel Hadar.

7. THE SECOND FEEDING

Hearing this astonishing praise of the God of Israel from the mouths of these Gentiles, Jesus was deeply touched. He found here not just surprise but belief. In contrast to the first feeding, here he himself took the initiative.

"Jesus called his disciples to him and said, 'I have compassion for these people ('misereor super turbam'; in the Greek: 'I am inwardly torn apart'); *they have already been with me three days and have nothing more to eat. I do not want to send them away hungry, or they may collapse on the*

way." (Mt 15:32) *"Some of them have come a long distance"* (Mk 8:3). ›A long distance‹ indicates not just physical distance but also spiritual: they had come from paganism.

Here was a real emergency. Jesus knew that it was time to return to Capernaum and he discussed things with his disciples. They were very embarrassed, *"for in this deserted area"* (Greek: eremia) there was nowhere to buy bread. Though Tabgha, where the first feeding took place, was also uninhabited, it was at least surrounded by villages. This hill on the eastern bank was far away from any inhabited places.

Tel Hadar

We have little to go by whether or not this hill was later visited by pilgrims (Tel Hadar, two miles north of Kursi provides the best place). In late Byzantine times it appears that people came here by boat from Tiberias. The Tel was then called ›Dodekathronos‹, referring perhaps to the seat-like blocks of rock which appear to be placed in a circle around the summit. The latest archaeological excavations have shown these stone blocks to be part of an earlier city wall, destroyed like many others by Assyrian attacks (733 B.C.).

In answer to Jesus' question as to how much bread they had at hand, his disciples could offer him seven loaves. Again he spoke the blessing over the bread (›Berakhah‹), he broke it and gave it to his disciples to distribute. In addition they had quite a number of small fish (›ikhthydia‹Mk 8:7)), most likely the so-called Kinneret sardines which are abundant in the waters of this area. Either they were bought from local fishermen or had been caught there. In the meantime someone could well have brought a boat from nearby Bethsaida.

Everyone had enough to eat and seven handled baskets (›spyris‹) full were collected, baskets which the people had brought with them. Although there is a clear distinction made between the kind of baskets used in the first feeding and in the second, hardly any translation

pays attention to it. The ›kophinoy‹ of the first feeding are large baskets, the ›spyridas‹ of the second feeding refer to panniers with handles as we find them in the floor mosaics of Kursi. In recalling the feedings Mark (8:19-20) uses the two distinctive terms on purpose. As the number twelve in the first feeding pointed to the twelve Tribes of Israel, so now the number seven was to indicate the seven heathen peoples (Deut 7:1b: *...the Hittites, Girgashites, Amorites, Canaanites, Perizzites, Hivites and Jebusites...* cf. Acts 13:191) , who had once inhabited the land but after its conquest had gradually disappeared or been

Contemporary baskets as found in the Judean Desert

driven out. As we have seen above, one of these biblical tribes who had been driven out, the Girgashites, had settled in this area. In the view of the Bible, the complete number of nations of the world was ten times seven. So this second feeding must have symbolically expressed that the messianic era had really begun. The gates giving entry to God's people now stood open to all nations.

"And they glorified the God of Israel" (Mt 15:31) Detail of the bronze door to the basilica in Tabgha

8. FOR ISRAEL THE SIGN OF JONAH

Jesus left the eastern shore and landed in Ma-gadan (Mt 15:39) near Capernaum where he had started his long journey. Mark names the landing place Dalmanutha (Mk 8:10) which some commentators take as an untranslated Aramaic expression meaning ›place of his stay‹. According to John the boat landed not far from Capernaum (Jn 6:17.21).

John combined the two feedings for a definite reason. For the most part he describes the first feeding but transfers the scene to the hill on the eastern shore, i.e., the location of the second feeding (Jn 6:1.3). According to the general tradition, the Walking on the Water followed the first feeding and so the fourth evangelist had to make a few small adjustments. In doing so he reveals a very intimate knowledge of the area. Sailing from east to west the disciples could not have had a head wind (Sharkiyeh) during the time before the Passover, so he avoids using the expression and mentions simply that a violent storm caused heavy seas (Jn 6:18). In addition, the traditional place where Jesus climbed into the boat to be with his disciples after the Walking on the Water was near Tabgha, so John lets the boat be some 25-30 stadia (approximately four miles) away from the place of the feeding (Jn 6:19). This is exactly the distance between Tel Hadar and Ma-gadan. One reason why John preferred to have the feeding on the mainly un-inhabited eastern shore might be that he wished to have a deserted landscape for his talk in the synagogue at Capernaum when he referred to the Manna in the desert (Jn 6:31). And Tabgha is no desert, but the other shore was a very desolate area. According to John the discourse on the Bread of Life comes in answer to the question :*"What miraculous sign then will you give that we may see it and believe you? What will you do?"* (Jn 6:30)

Also according to both Matthew and Mark, Jesus is bothered on his arrival at the western shore by the question of a sign.

"The Pharisees and Sadducees came to Jesus and tested him by asking him to show them a sign from heaven. He replied, '...a wicked and adulterous generation looks for a miraculous sign, but none will be given it except the sign of Jonah'" (Mt 16:1-4; Mk 8:11-12).

What was his point? What is the sign of Jonah? We find the best answer in a saying ›Logion‹ noted by Luke. *"As the crowds increased, Jesus said, 'This is a wicked generation. It asks for a miraculous sign, but none will be given it except the sign of Jonah. For as Jonah was a sign to the Ninevites, so also will the Son of Man be to this generation. ...The men of Nineveh will stand up at the judgment with this generation and condemn it; for they repented at the preaching of Jonah, and now one greater than Jonah is here'"* (Lk 11:29-32). The book of Jonah is a parable by a great theologian of Israel, who wants to say that Yahweh, their God, is not just the God of Israel but of all nations and cares for everyone. The sign of Jonah is the conversion of Nineveh, the pagan capital of the Assyrians who had destroyed the northern kingdom. Jonah, a prophet of this northern kingdom (2K 14:25), would have been familiar to the Galileans since his home town Gath Hepher was only a few miles north of Nazareth.

Jonah in the fish (early Christian oil lamp)

This mention of the Sign of Jonah can be seen as the fruit of what Jesus had learnt on his long journey and with this, one of the periods in the life of Jesus comes to an end. In Capernaum he had tried to bring his word to the people by assimilating to the most influential Torah school in Israel, that of the Pharisees. He had not been successful. Wherever he tried to find new ways to interiorize the Torah, he met with opposition. The miracles which he performed won him the people's amazement and requests for more, but only very few believed.

Amongst the Gentiles, on the other hand, he found an unexpected faith. With the sign of Jonah he wanted to tell his people: The Kingdom of Heaven is offered first of all to you. You do not accept it but the Gentiles will. This shall be a sign to you that the messianic kingdom has come. It is the mystery of Israel - God's chosen people - that the sign of Jonah holds true to this day.

Paul, who as a Jew suffered under this mystery of his people, tried to explain the hidden plan of God: *"A hardening has come upon part of Israel, until the full number of the Gentiles has come in. And so all Israel will be saved, as it is written: The deliverer will come from Zion..."* (Romans 11:25-26).

86

THE JOURNEY TO CAESAREA PHILIPPI:

CHANGING MESSIANIC ATTITUDES

1. CRISIS IN CAPERNAUM

After the sharp rejection of the Pharisees' demand for a sign (Mt 16) both Mark and Matthew at once start on the third journey which brings Jesus and his followers to the majestic mountain range of Hermon. We can better understand the urgency for this journey when we realize that after the feeding of the multitude on the eastern side of the lake a crisis occurred in Capernaum which involved not only the Pharisees but also Jesus' own disciples. The account of this is in the fourth Gospel. Even though it may be assumed that Jesus' discourse in the synagogue of Capernaum and the reaction of his audience have been strongly worked up in the redaction by the evangelist, one does sense a crisis of faith which has caused a marked thinning-out of the number of his disciples.

Jesus' discourse on the Bread from Heaven (Jn 6:26-59) caused much confusion. Following the first feeding he was offered the leadership of the messianic movement, but he refused it and fled to the mountains (Jn 6:15). This prophet, who had given rise to so much hope, suddenly seems to get lost in unreal mystical speculations which had little to do with the hope of Israel in its contemporary political situation. *"I am the living bread that came down from heaven. If anyone eats of this bread, he will live for ever. This bread is my flesh, which I will give for the life of the world... For my flesh is real food and my blood is real drink."* (Jn 6:51.55).

If these or similar words really go back to the historical Jesus, it is easy to understand the indignation of his followers. *"How can this man give us his flesh to eat"* (Jn 6:52). Even worse for Jewish ears would have been the word to "drink his blood." Their reaction was understandable. *"This is hard teaching. Who can accept it?"* (Jn 6:60) *"From this time many of his disciples turned back and no longer followed him"* (Jn 6:66). Gradually he seemed to lose the majority of his disciples.

Only the Twelve remained. *"'Do you also want to leave?' Jesus asked the Twelve. Simon Peter answered him, 'Lord, to whom shall we go? You have the words of eternal life. We believe and know that you are the Holy One of God'"* (Jn 6:67-69).

2. THE JOURNEY BY BOAT TO BETHSAIDA

Mark tries to explain how the closest disciples came to believe by recounting a long journey to the north. This journey began by sailing from Capernaum to Bethsaida. *"Then he left them, got back into the boat and crossed to the other side"* (Mk 8:13).

The journey begins with a strange remark. *"The disciples had forgotten to bring bread, except for the one loaf they had with them in the boat"* (Mk 8:14). This one loaf, the writer intimates, was Christ himself, a

1. ›*To Bethsaida on the other shore*‹ (Mk 6:45; 8:13.22)
The entry and the exit of the Jordan into and from the lake form an imaginary line which determined whether a location was ›on this side‹ or ›on the other side‹ of the lake. Both the Gospels and the contemporary Josephus Flavius take it in this way.
"*From Panion at the grotto the visible course of the Jordan starts, which crosses the marshes and flats of Lake Semachonites* (now the drained Lake Hula) *and 120 Stades further on south of the town of (Bethsaida-) Julias flows through the Lake of Gennesaret and after a long way through the desert flows out into the Asphalt Sea* (Dead Sea)" B.J. 3,515.

2. **On the foundation of Julias:**
"*The Tetrarch Philip raised the village Bethsaida on Lake Gennesaret to the dignity of a city (polis), on the grounds of the number of its inhabitants and its strong position, and named it Julias, after the daughter of the Emperor*" Ant. 18,28.

fact which the disciples simply could not understand. Here is a possible parallel to John's reflection on Jesus as the Bread of Life. Jesus himself seems to point in that direction: "'*Why are you talking about having no bread? Do you still not see or understand? ...And don't you remember? When I broke the five loaves for the five thousand, how many baskets full of pieces did you pick up?' 'Twelve,' they replied. 'And when I broke the seven loaves for the four thousand, how many panniers full of pieces did you pick up?' They answered, 'Seven.' He said to them, 'Do you still not understand'?*" (Mk 8:17-22). He meant "As long as you have me, the Bread of Life, with you, what could you possibly lack?" But it was just beyond their comprehension.

What was even less clear to them, and what made this journey of re-education so necessary, lay hidden in the initial warning of Jesus: "'*Be careful,' Jesus warned them. 'Watch out for the yeast of the Pharisees and that of Herod'*" (Mk 8:15).

What was in question here was fundamentally the disciples' conception of the Messiah. The Pharisees, and in particular the Zealots who were a fanatical offshoot of the Pharisees, saw Israel's redemption in the struggle against Rome, while the Herodian dynasty offered the hope that friendship with Rome would result in peace and contentment.

›The Boat‹ a contemporary fishing boat, a singular find, was recovered from the lake a few years ago after some dry years made the water level recede drastically. Today it stands in a specially built basin in a chemical solution that is to harden the 2,000-year-old wood and preserve it.

3. BETWEEN GAMLA AND TIBERIAS

The boat which was to take Jesus and the Twelve disciples from Capernaum to Bethsaida sailed between Tiberias in the southwest and Gamla in the northeast. They represented two opposing political attitudes of that particular period.

Not yet ten years had passed since Tiberias had been founded by Herod Antipas. Devout Jews considered it unclean and avoided it because it had been built upon a graveyard. At the death of Herod the Great (37-4 B.C.) the Kingdom of Judea was divided into four tetrarchies. Two were inherited by Herod's son Antipas: Galilee and Perea. The tetrarchy Batanea, Trachonitis and Gaulanitis was inherited by his brother Philip. The Jordan river formed the frontier between those two. Herod Antipas was a very ambitious ruler. Prodded by his unlawful wife, Herodias, his ambition was to achieve the official title of ›king‹, but he never succeeded. Still, his subjects (and sometimes the evangelists too) called him so. For this reason he was utterly loyal to Rome and careful to win the Emperor's favor.

Philip was a more modest man and well-respected by his subjects. He became particularly popular, according to Josephus, for he always took a folding chair on his journeys throughout his territory, which he set up each time he was asked to make a legal decision (Ant. 18,107). He had promoted the large village of Bethsaida to the status of a city (polis) soon after his entering into office and had named it Julias in honor of the Emperor's daughter (Ant 18,28).

The Herodian vassals and their supporters served the Roman empire and fought to consolidate Roman hegemony over these eastern Mediterranean lands.

Gamla, the neighboring town to Bethsaida, represented a completely opposite political line. Like an eyrie, Gamla was poised on a rocky ridge protected on each side by deep sweeping valleys. With its patriotic ideals this place held sway over a large portion of the Jewish people around the lake. Jehuda of Gamla, who was a Pharisean scholar, together with Rabbi Tzadok, a Pharisee too, founded the Zealot movement in A.D. 6. His family developed into a dynasty that

The synagogue of Gamla

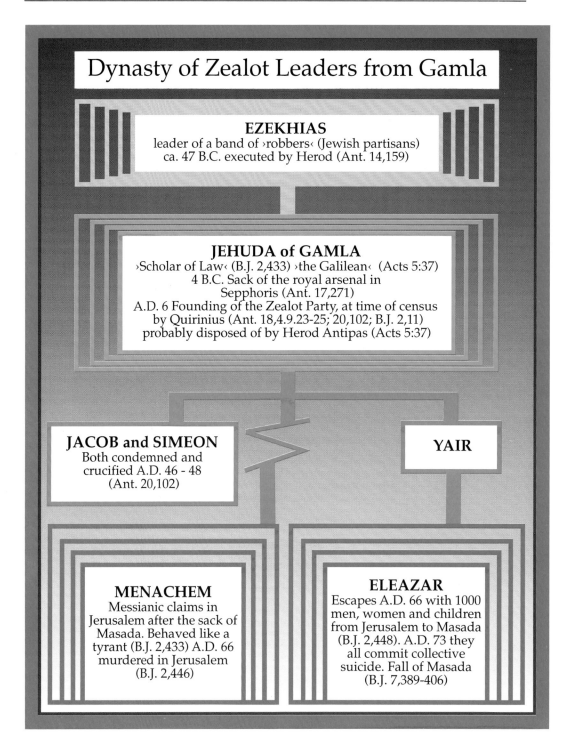

Dynasty of Zealot Leaders from Gamla

EZEKHIAS
leader of a band of ›robbers‹ (Jewish partisans)
ca. 47 B.C. executed by Herod (Ant. 14,159)

JEHUDA of GAMLA
›Scholar of Law‹ (B.J. 2,433) ›the Galilean‹ (Acts 5:37)
4 B.C. Sack of the royal arsenal in
Sepphoris (Ant. 17,271)
A.D. 6 Founding of the Zealot Party, at time of census
by Quirinius (Ant. 18,4.9.23-25; 20,102; B.J. 2,11)
probably disposed of by Herod Antipas (Acts 5:37)

JACOB and SIMEON
Both condemned and
crucified A.D. 46 - 48
(Ant. 20,102)

YAIR

MENACHEM
Messianic claims in
Jerusalem after the sack of
Masada. Behaved like a
tyrant (B.J. 2,433) A.D. 66
murdered in Jerusalem
(B.J. 2,446)

ELEAZAR
Escapes A.D. 66 with 1000
men, women and children
from Jerusalem to Masada
(B.J. 2,448). A.D. 73 they
all commit collective
suicide. Fall of Masada
(B.J. 7,389-406)

formed the leaders of the movement of the Zealots until it was defeated in the siege at Masada. Already Jehuda's father Ezekias (Hiskiya) had been a patriot, who as leader of a band of guerrillas had risen against the Romans and their allies in the district of Trachonitis. He was eventually captured by the young Herod and executed.

Jehuda of Gamla taught a very radical theocracy: God alone was the ruler of Israel, not the Roman Emperor. And therefore one ought not to pay him taxes. In the Acts of the Apostles it is written of Jehuda: *"Judas the Galilean appeared in the days of the census and led a band of people in revolt. He too was killed, and all his followers were scattered"* (Acts 5:37). It seems that Herod Antipas was probably responsible for his execution. Two of his sons, Jacob and Simon, were crucified under the procurator Tiberius Alexander (A.D. 46-48). In a raid on Masada in A.D. 66, Menahem, his son or grandson, seized weapons, entered Jerusalem as though he were the Messiah himself and gained control over the rebels. He was finally murdered by the opposition.

Chares and Joseph, ›the Son of the Midwife‹, who lived in the spirit of Jehuda, led the battle of Gamla (A.D. 66-67) with exceptional tenacity that eventually ended in collective suicide. In order not to fall into the hands of the Romans, after a long siege the defenders of Gamla threw themselves down the cliffs thus avoiding captivity (B.J. 4,79-80). Eleazar, also a grandson of Jehuda of Gamla, was leader of the Zealots on Masada. This entire zealot movement was much influenced by the messianic expectations. A political Messiah was awaited who would lead his troops from victory to victory against Rome.

Andrew of Bethsaida most certainly understood it in these terms, when, after meeting Jesus, he whispered into the ear of his brother Simon: *"'We have found the Messiah' (that is, the Christ)"* (Jn 1:41). One of Jesus' disciples was specifically named a Zealot: *"Simon, the Zealot"* (Mk 3:18; Lk 6:15). He could possibly have come from Gamla. Judas Iscariot was also another whose messianic hopes were similar to those of the Zealots. More or less all the apostles shared a similar view of the Messiah. This is hardly surprising considering how close to each other Gamla and Bethsaida were situated. From Bethsaida came the apostles of first rank (Peter and Andrew, James and John, Philip). A re-education of the Twelve was urgently needed.

4. THE HEALING OF A BLIND MAN IN BETHSAIDA

Andrew's home town, Bethsaida, was situated on a hill on the eastern bank of the Jordan, which flowed into the lake about one mile further downstream. At that time the river Jordan did not sweep in a large loop as it does today, but it flowed straight into a shallow lagoon before reaching the lake itself, so that a small part of Bethsaida lay on the west bank of the Jordan river (Bethsaida in Galilee cf. Jn 12:21). The Apostle Philip apparently had his home there. One can still see the original bed of the river Jordan.

The disciples in the company of Jesus steered their boat through the lagoon with its abundance of fish and rowed upriver which was navigable up to Bethsaida.

On landing they passed a rich spring on their way into the town. *"They came to Bethsaida, and some people brought a blind man and begged Jesus to touch him. He took the blind man by the hand and led him outside the village. When he had put spittle on the man's eyes and put his hands on him, Jesus asked, 'Do you see anything?' He looked up and said, 'I see people; they look like trees walking around.' Once more Jesus put his hands on the man's eyes. Then his eyes were opened, his sight was restored and he saw everything clearly"* (Mk 8:22-25). The man was healed in stages, something without parallel in Mark's Gospel. The exegetes are right in saying that Jesus wanted to perform a symbolic act like the prophets often did.

The pond with water from the spring of Bethsaida

Shortly before this Jesus had told the twelve: *"Do you have eyes but fail to see...?"* (Mk 8:18). Their inner eyes were blind as that blind man's eyes had been. By the gradual healing of the blind man Jesus wanted to give a sign to his disciples to show how a person comes to faith. Belief is not a sudden recognition, but a gradual process toward a deeper understanding. For this reason Jesus took them out of their immediate environment and journeyed with them far up to Caesarea Philippi that he may initiate them into what he saw as his messianic mission.

The place of the healing near Bethsaida is marked today by a memorial stone on which two eyes have been chiselled, one half-closed and the other open brightly.

5. PETER - FAITH AND RESISTANCE

When Jesus reached the foot of the majestic Mount Hermon after a long day's journey he turned to his disciples with the question *"'Who do people say I am?' They replied, 'Some say John the Baptist; others say Elijah; and still others, one of the prophets'"* (Mk 8:27-28). Then came the decisive question to the disciples: *"'But what about you?' he asked. 'Who do you say I am?' Peter answered, 'You are the Christ'"* (Mk 8:29). It was out, the declaration. They had been together for so long, yet no one had dared mention it openly in front of Jesus although they had often whispered it among themselves. Now they were bewildered by his peculiar order: *"Jesus warned them not to tell anyone about him"* (Mk 8:30).

This secretiveness over the title of Messiah may seem strange.

Having discovered the location of Gamla some twenty years ago and its proximity to Jesus' sphere of activity, it is easier to understand the reason for this anxiety. Jesus wanted to say "Tell no one, you will only be misunderstood." The idea of the Messiah in the northern section of the lake was strongly colored by revolutionary militancy.

When Jesus reached the foot of the majestic Mount Hermon after a long day's journey...

Now the time had come for Jesus to present his own outlook. Jesus had sought his Father's will through prayer and he had reached an understanding of Messiah which sounded quite different from the expectations of his disciples. Reflection on "the Songs of the Suffering Servant" in the prophecies of Isaiah must certainly have played an important part.

"He then began to teach them that the Son of Man must suffer many things and be rejected by the elders, chief priests and teachers of the law, and that he must be killed and after three days rise again. He spoke plainly about this" (Mk 8:31-32a).

It must have been like a cold shower on the Messianic enthusiasm of the disciples. That such should be the lot of the Messiah was both inconceivable and intolerable. Peter, who had just had the courage to profess Jesus to be the Messiah and had been praised accordingly (Mt 16:17) now stood up to Jesus. He took Jesus aside to present the view of the disciples. He *"began to rebuke him"* (Mk 8:32). Matthew elaborates somewhat more: *"'Never, Lord!' he said. 'This shall never happen to you!'"* (Mt 16:22). Jesus finds himself obstructed by those most faithful to him. What follows is a dramatic confrontation of determination on one side and wishful thinking on the other.

"But when Jesus turned and looked at his disciples, he rebuked Peter. 'Get behind me, Satan!' he said. 'You do not have in mind the things of God, but the things of men'" (Mk 8:33). That was exactly the problem: The popular image of the Messiah was the way they all saw him. Not that Jesus

96

was not himself tempted to see himself as a triumphant Messiah. The various possibilities in taking on the role of the Messiah had been evident to him after his baptism in the Jordan but he decisively rejected them, seeing them as temptations of Satan. But now temptation lurked again from the direction of his closest fellow-workers: to follow a different path from the one his Father's will had marked out. Just as decisively as before he flung his refusal against them.

It must have been a painful shock to Peter to be referred to as ›Satan‹ by his beloved master. It was difficult too for the others, who had been hiding behind Peter. The next pericope starts *"After six days..."* It must have been six days of tension between the master and his disciples. Surely little was spoken. However, they remained with him and this brought healing.

6. ON THE HIGH MOUNTAIN

"After six days Jesus took Peter, James and John with him and led them up a high mountain, where they were all alone" (Mk 9,2). They were the three key figures amongst the Twelve. Through the experience which is called the Transfiguration they were introduced to the mystery of the divine incarnation of Christ, the God-Man. Only in this way could their inner blindness be healed. They had to see and hear.

Which was this high mountain? A very ancient local tradition claimed Tabor to be the mountain of the Transfiguration. However, this presents great difficulties. First of all, Tabor lies too far away to fit into the story. The main problem, however, lies in the fact that at that time Mount Tabor was populated (Ant. 13,396) and a Hasmonean fortress stood on its summit. The fortified mountain had to be conquered by the Romans in the great Jewish War in the year A.D. 67 (B.J. 4,54-61).

I support the view of many commentators that the *"high mountain"* was Mount Hermon. This tradition, also very old, is testified by the great Church historian Eusebius (265-340). Mount Hermon was generally considered in the local tradition as a holy mountain. (The Hebrew word Hermon can be translated as: ›The Mountain Set Apart‹.) The Second Letter of Peter, 1:18 also confirms this. *"We ourselves heard this voice that came from heaven when we were with him on the holy mountain."* The *"high mountain"* (Mk 9:2) need not necessarily be the summit of Hermon, but simply one of the peaks in the Hermon range.

Through the mystical experience of the Transfiguration the three disciples were able to sense something of the hidden nature of their master, the God-Man. There was much more to him than they could ever experience through daily contact with him. The appearance of Moses and Elijah, two great figures in the history of Israel, indicated to them that their beloved Rabbi stood in the line of the great prophets of Israel. It was extremely important that the faith of these three should, through the vision, be rooted so deeply as to enable them to stand fast at the sight of Jesus' utter self-abasement in the Garden of Gethsemane.

Were the other nine rather upset by the preferential treatment of the three? Coming down the Holy Mount they found the other disciples involved in an argument with some scholars. Through historical sources (Josephus) we know of large numbers of Jews in and around Caesarea Philippi.

The fact that the disciples were not able to heal the epileptic youth (Mk 9:17-29) shows that real depth to their faith was still lacking.

7. RETURN TO CAPERNAUM

After these stirring days in the north Jesus returned to Galilee. *"They left that place and passed through Galilee. Jesus did not want anyone to know where they were, because he was teaching his disciples"* (Mk 9:30). Very soon he would be back in Capernaum where he would have little chance of talking closely to his disciples. He therefore took advantage of a quiet moment on the edge of Galilee, possibly near Lake Hula, to acquaint the Twelve once again with the messianic role as he had come to understand it.

He had reflected much on it and even shortly before the descent from the high mountain he told the three: *"Why then is it written that the Son of Man must suffer much and be rejected?"* (Mk 9,12b cf. Isaiah 52:13- 53,12; Ps 22:2-20). Now he said to them: *"The Son of Man is going to be betrayed into the hands of men. They will kill him, and after three days he will rise"* (Mk 9:31).

The comment by the Evangelist after this second prediction of the Passion, is characteristic of the apostles' attitude: *"But they did not understand what he meant and were afraid to ask him about it"* (Mk 9:32). They were still feeling the effects of the sharp rebuke they had received on the first occasion. What they now realized quite clearly was that they must not question this point any more.

Zeal was not lacking, particularly with John and James, the Sons of Thunder. Their zeal, however, easily led to jealousy. A typical example of this was the meeting with an unknown miracle-worker who came their way on their return journey (Mk 9:38-41). This man was a self-made disciple and tried to cast out devils in Jesus' name. In his excessive zeal John wanted to forbid him doing so. "Either you join us or you leave your hands off of this!" When he later reported the incident, Jesus displayed great tolerance in his reply: *"'Do not stop him,' Jesus said. 'No one who does a miracle in my name can in the next moment say anything bad about me, for whoever is not against us is for us'"* (Mk 9: 39-40).

At last they reached Capernaum, his home town (Mk 9:33). Jesus, deeply engrossed in thought, had gone on ahead of the disciples. Now, as they all sat together in the house of Peter's mother-in-law, *"he asked them: 'What were you arguing about on the road?' But they kept quiet because on the way they had argued about who was the greatest"* (Mk 9:33-34).

Was this the end result of this journey of instruction, after Jesus had gone to such length to explain the seriousness of the situation? What obviously interested them most of all was the question of status in the circle of disciples. One can well imagine Jesus near to despair at this moment.

With great patience he gathered the Twelve around him and sitting down *"said: 'If anyone wants to be first, he must be the very last, and the servant of all.' He took a little child and set him in the midst of them"* (Mk 9:35-36). Jesus emphasized that only serving one's fellow-being and in particular the little ones would give them a share in his work and in that of his Father who had sent him.

Surely Jesus must have been disheartened as he sat in the house of Peter that evening. How could the Messiah establish the Kingdom of God on earth with such human characters as he had at his disposal? Can't we observe similar shortcomings in the Church officials of to-day? And yet in such failures we also find an encouraging note for us all. It was with this human stock after all that Jesus conquered the world. We are probably no better, but neither are we much worse than the apostles. Perhaps he can do something with us as well. It is, we know, God's work, not ours.

...they left that place and passed through Galilee ...(looking back from the Hula Valley)

FROM GALILEE
TO
JERUSALEM

1. DEPARTURE FROM GALILEE

Jesus' time in Galilee was slowly coming to an end. In Caesarea Philippi, Peter had been first to confess his faith in his master as the Messiah. He also took the initiative to proclaim Jesus as the Saviour to both his own people and the Gentiles. In Caesarea Maritima Peter witnessed before the family of the God-fearing centurion Cornelius by giving testimony of Jesus' activities in Galilee. *"You know what has happened throughout the land of the Jews, beginning in Galilee after the baptism that John preached - how God anointed Jesus of Nazareth with the Holy Spirit and power, and how he went around doing good and healing all who were under the power of the devil, because God was with him"* (Acts 10:37-38).

Capernaum had been chosen as the center of Jesus' work in Galilee. There he lived with Peter, to whom he entrusted the care of his flock, despite his impulsive character.

The house of Peter (a drawing based on the archaeological finds in Capernaum) - Outside the courtyard passed the road, which after branching off from the Via Maris led through the town towards the lake. The doorstep into the courtyard is still visible. The front door led into the room where Jesus taught. The paralytic (Mk 2:1-12) was carried by the four men upstairs. The roof was opened and part of the wall was broken so that the paralytic could be lowered on his mat down in front of Jesus' feet.

The choice of this particular place had led to dissension with his own clan of Natzoreans. He was not prepared to put himself at the disposition of his relatives for the sake of their self-centered messianic aspirations.Their exclusiveness, certainly influenced by the Essenes, was far too narrow, while the liberating message of the Gospel was meant to be for all.

Therefore, during his stay in Capernaum, he tried to enter into dialogue with the Pharisees, who were then the most influential religious group among the Jews. He had friends among the Pharisees, especially those who followed the Hillel line of thought. Simon the Pharisee invited Jesus to a meal in his home. Rabbi Nicodemus, whose family according to recent Jewish research, also came from Galilee, had a profound theological conversation with Jesus one night. But it was precisely these pious men with their insistence upon the Traditions of the Fathers who felt they could not accept Jesus' interpretation of the Torah.

Reconstructed houses in ancient Katzrin on the Golan Hights

The ordinary people of Capernaum were full of admiration for Jesus' message and *"asked each other, 'What is this? A new teaching - and with authority'"* (Mk 1:27). The Pharisees gradually began to see Jesus' popularity as dangerous, and soon their resentment developed into enmity.

Since the Pharisees in the northern townships around the lake were under the strong influence of the Zealot spirit emanating from nearby Gamla, Jesus must have soon realized that his contacts with the Pharisees would eventually come to nothing. In turn, the Pharisees became aware that this man from Nazareth, who had performed so many astonishing signs which drew large crowds of people under his spell, was no candidate for the Messiah they were waiting for who could free their country from the Roman overlordship. They dropped Jesus.

As the re-education of the disciples, which Jesus had striven to achieve on his last journey north, had been marked by incomprehension, the end result of Jesus' efforts in Galilee must have been disappointing. This disappointment is expressed in a saying (Logion) preserved for us by Matthew:

"Then Jesus began to denounce the towns in which most of his deeds had been performed, because they did not repent. 'Woe to you, Korazin! Woe to you, Bethsaida! ...And you, Capernaum, will you be lifted up to the skies? No, you will go down to the depths'" (Mt 11:20-23). He had invested so much goodwill in this corner by the lake, which is appropriately named the ›Evangelical Triangle‹. The inhabitants had responded with admiration and astonishment, but his efforts had failed to lead them to belief in his real mission. After the distressing crisis of faith in Capernaum the large crowds that had gathered there during the initial months of the ›Galilean Spring‹ stayed away. Only the Twelve remained and even they only understood him partially.

In addition the danger posed by the ruler of the territory, Herod Antipas, became ever more apparent. Luke tells of an occurrence which best fits into the time shortly before Jesus' departure from Galilee:

"At that time some Pharisees came to Jesus and said to him, 'Leave this place and go somewhere else. Herod wants to kill you.' He replied: 'Go tell that fox, I will drive out demons and heal people today and to-morrow, and on the third day I will reach my goal.' In any case, I must keep going today and to-morrow and the next day - for surely no prophet can die outside Jerusalem!'" (Lk 13:31-33).

It is quite plausible that these Pharisees were friends of Jesus who meant well with their warnings. Or did they? We have already seen that Herod kept a close watch on what happened around Jesus, whom he suspected of being John the Baptist come back to life. In the case of Jesus, who was his subject (as had been the case with John the Baptist), he was highly suspicious of the great crowds that gathered around such a charismatic figure. One small spark and a revolution would be at hand. A threat of death "delivered" by the Pharisees, whom Herod could not tolerate anyhow, might have the desired effect.

So it is not difficult to imagine that Antipas and certain Pharisees who hated him may have joined forces. For both wished this undesirable mischief-maker removed from their territory. Earlier on we hear of an "unholy alliance" against Jesus. Mark states: *"Then the Pharisees*

...shortly afterwards he decided to depart from Galilee...

went out and began to plot with the Herodians how they might kill Jesus" (Mk 3:6). Jesus realized that the tentacles of the murderer of John the Baptist were creeping closer to himself.

His reply amounted to a challenge. With tranquil courage he faced the threat coming from ›that fox‹ who surveyed the whole region from his castle in Tiberias. He must have been aware that the hour of his death was approaching, but that it would neither overtake him in Galilee nor in the desert castle of Machaerus, but in Jerusalem. He would definitely leave Herod's territory, but at a time decided on by him, once his work was done.

Although Jesus himself determined the end of his ministry in Galilee in complete freedom, he was nonetheless well aware of the danger from that "scheming fox." So shortly afterwards he must have decided to depart from Galilee.

THE BATANEA TRADITIONS

1. In the Syriac Church an ancient tradition lived on that Jesus had come on his flight from Herod Antipas into Syrian territory, to which Batanea was added after the death of Agrippa II (ca. 100).

Ephrem the Syrian (306-373) reports: *"Jacob, the son of Isaac, was a shepherd. He had to flee from his brother, who was older than himself, and so was put in charge of Syrian sheep. The same happened also to Jesus, the teacher of Jews, who were his first sheep. But when he was persecuted by Herod the King, he had to flee and in this way became also a shepherd to the Syrian brethren"* (CSCO vol. 292, t.6, Ste. 40, 25 par 59. cf par.. 25,61).

2. **Egeria's pilgrimage** (ca. 384) to the grave of Job in the land of Uz near Karnajim in Batanea.

• She reports about her motivation for the pilgrimage: *"After a certain time I wanted to travel in the land of Uz (Ausitis, Job 1:1) to visit the tomb of Job to pray there. I noticed that many holy monks came to Jerusalem from there to pray at the holy places. Their reports on those places stirred in me the longing to reach them myself... there are eight stages on the journey from Jerusalem to Carnayim (Carneas), which describes itself as the town of Job"* (13,1-2). The place is today called ›Sheikh el Miskin‹ (the Unfortunate Sheikh) by the Moslems who have picked up this Christian tradition.

• Egeria's visit to Aenon by Salim: On her pilgrimage Egeria passed through Samaria with the monk-guides and got down into the Jordan valley at Mehola. She reports: *"On that road I saw a lovely and attractive valley full of vineyards and orchards, because of the plentiful fresh water in that place"* (13,2).

Egeria noticed in the middle of the plain a small hill (today Tel Shalim) which has around it foundations of a strong wall. On the hill stood a church. In reply to her questions about it, she was told that this had been Salem, the town of the king Melchizedek. The priest of the place showed her the town and pointed out the road where Abraham had met Melchizedek. She continued: *"Then I remembered that it was written that St. John had baptized at Aenon near Salim (Jn 3:23) and I asked him if that place were far away. Then that holy priest said 'It was only 200 paces distant. If you so wish, I'll walk you there. The good and rich water supply for this village comes from that spring.' I thanked him and asked him to take us to that place. And so that is what happened. We began to go along the plain of this charming valley until we reached a delightful orchard, where he showed me a spring in the middle with plentiful fresh water, which formed quite a brook. In front of the spring itself was a sort of a pool where apparently John the Baptist baptized. Then the holy priest said to us 'This garden is called to this very day ›Kepos tu hagiu Johanni‹ which means in Latin ›hortus sancti Johannis‹ (the Garden of John). Many brothers, holy monks, come from various places to bathe there...* (15,1-4).

- Egeria continues her journey to Batanea. The priest went on to recount to Egeria that the people of the place were baptized at Easter. As a parting gift she was offered fruit from the ›Garden of John‹. Thereupon Egeria's party of pilgrims went along the Jordan, crossed it and visited Tishbeh, the home of the prophet Elijah. They were shown a cave there, in which the prophet was reputed to have stayed. She goes on: *"When we went on, I saw to our left a splendid valley. The valley was extremely big and let a great deal of water into the Jordan. We noticed a monastery of a brother, that is of a monk, in that valley.*
  Since I am pretty curious, I asked what valley it was where that holy monk had built himself this monastery. I thought he must have had a reason for doing so, Then the holy men, who accompanied us and were familiar with the area said: 'This is the Valley of Corra, where the prophet Elijah from Tishbeh had stayed in the time of King Ahab, during the Famine. At the command of God, a raven brought him food and he drank from the river (1K 17:1). The river is the Corra" (16, 2-3).

3. The river Kerith, which according to the Hebrew flows from the east into the Jordan (1K 17:3.5) was in fact called Corra in the Greek Septuagint. Today one of the three rivers which make up the Yarmuk is still called Charir. So we can safely state that the biblical name for the Yarmuk was Kerith. It was the Greeks of the Decapolis who named it Yarmuk (Hieromax), from the hieros muchos, or holy ravine.
   After her visit to the traditional tomb of Job in the region of Karnajim (a page is missing here from the original text) Egeria returned to Jerusalem.

2. IN JUDEA BEYOND THE JORDAN

Matthew (Mt 19:1) and Mark (Mk 10:1) inform us that Jesus had left Galilee with his disciples and crossed over *"into the region of Judea beyond the Jordan."* It is unlikely that this area was Perea as is sometimes claimed. For the tetrarchy of Perea was, like Galilee, within the jurisdiction of Herod Antipas. Probably it was there that the Baptist was captured by Herod's henchmen and put in custody in the cliff fortress of Machaerus in the mountains east of the Dead Sea. Moreover, Perea was never referred to as ›Judea on the other side of the Jordan‹. That expression more likely referred to another area, Batanea, as we have already seen in Chapter 1, a former Israelite area of settlement (the tribe of Manasseh).

At the time of Herod the Great and his sons, Judea comprised Judea proper in the south with Idumea as well as the northern territories, including Galilee, Gaulanitis and Batanea. During the revolt of A.D. 66-70 Josephus considered the northern region on the far side of the Jordan as Judean (B.J. 5,56). From the previous century on, many Jews had settled there upon returning from the Babylonian and Persian diaspora.

The Jewish tribe from Ecbatane cared for law and order in that area. These Babylonian Jews, also named the ›Batanean Clan‹, stood on a very good footing with the tetrarch Philip. At the time of Jesus, Jakimos, the son of Zamaris, was prince of Batanea. Josephus calls him "a man of shining valour" (Ant. 17,23-31).

After leaving Galilee, Jesus entered this Jewish region on the other side of the Jordan. Matthew says that *"large crowds followed him, and he healed them there"* (Mt 19:2). Once again a fruitful, undisturbed period of activity followed. It was no longer possible for the unpredictable ›fox‹ from Tiberias to throw his sinister shadow over Jesus. He was no longer obliged to avoid the gathering of enthusiastic crowds as he had been during the last few months in Galilee. Mark reports: *"Again crowds of people came to him, and as was his custom, he taught them"* (Mk 10:1b).

The fourth Evangelist makes a similar remark. According to John, Jesus and his group came into this area after their flight from Jerusalem following the Feast of Hanukah (Dedication) in the winter of A.D. 29.

"Then Jesus went back across the Jordan to the place where John had been baptizing in the early days. Here he stayed and many people came to him. They said: 'Though John never performed a miraculous sign, all that John said about this man was true.' And in that place many believed in Jesus" (Jn 10:40-42).

Josephus reports that John's ministry in that area had political repercussions in later years. When Philip the tetrarch died without heirs in Bethsaida-Julias in the year 34 A.D. and was buried in the mausoleum he had built, his half-brother Antipas had hoped that the Emperor Tiberius would give him that tetrarchy as well. He had already incorporated the majority of the troops from Batanea into his own army. However, a border disagreement arose between him and the Nabatean King Aretas. During the ensuing battle in the region of Gaulanitis Antipas suffered a severe defeat. The cause lay in the fact that the soldiers who had come from the tetrarchy of Philip refused to fight and consequently fled (Ant. 18,114). The reason for desertion was resentment which had continued to seethe in the minds of these soldiers since Antipas had treacherously murdered John the Baptist in prison eight years before. Josephus states that many pious Jews saw this defeat as the just punishment by God for the murder of the prophet (Ant. 18,5,2;116).

It has been supposed with good reason that pious Essene Jews also settled in this autonomous region of Batanea. According to the 'Copper Scroll of Qumran' they seem to have had a monastic centre there, a ›Kokhlit‹. Was this perhaps the ›land of Damascus‹ to which the Qumran scrolls referred as their place of refuge?

It can also be supposed that the previously mentioned esoteric clan of the ›Babylonian Jews‹, who never mixed with the other Jews, was a syncretistic sect blending Jewish and Persian elements. I think we should see in them the Mandaeans, who were influenced by ideas of the Essenes, Natzoreans and John the Baptist. Later they appear to have left this Jordan region and returned to their land of origin by the Persian Gulf, probably at the time of Bar-Kochba (ca. A.D. 135). Today there are still a few of these Mandaeans living in that region who regard John the Baptist as their great leader and Jesus as a false prophet. The Yarmuk which forms the southern border of the Batanea was until recently called by the Bedouins ›Shiryat el Mandireh‹ (the river of the Mandaeans). After this clan of Bataneans had disappeared from the region (cf. Ant. 18,106) and from their area of settlement, Ecbatane, which found its way into the local name Batanea (or in Jn 1:28, Bethaneia), the ancient name of Bashan or Basanitis reappears in the literary sources.

The remark in the fourth Gospel *"and many came to believe in him"* seems to refer to a situation which existed at the end of the first century when this Gospel was written. We know that at this time flourishing Jewish-Christian communities existed there. Some exegetes even suspect that the basic text of John's Gospel originated there.

3. THE BATANEA. THE FIRST STAGE ON THE WAY UP TO JERUSALEM

We might try to imagine the route Jesus took to the other side of the Jordan after his decision to leave the increasingly dangerous tetrarchy of Antipas.

Jesus may have taken a boat from Capernaum and sailed across the lake towards the area of Tel Hadar, where the second Feeding of the Multitude had taken place. From here a Roman road, traces of which can still be found near the modern Moshav Ramot, lead up toward the Golan Heights. It was winter and the first rainfalls had very likely allowed grass to sprout in between the black basalt rocks. After reaching the heights the small group around Jesus enjoyed the magnificent view of the lake and the surrounding villages. In the far north, majestic Mount Hermon, covered with a snow-white cloak, would have dominated the entire scene. Peace and tranquillity reigned in the land of the mild Jewish tetrarch, Philip, a territory Jesus was now visiting.

The Roman road avoided the deep Rukkad gully and passed over a bridge north of the beautiful Rukkad Falls into the Jewish area of the autonomous Batanea. Certainly news of Jesus' mighty deeds had already preceded him (cf. Mt 4:24).

Mark tells us of three events which took place in Judea beyond the Jordan. In the light of what has just been said of this region, it is easier to understand their actual context.

There is the report of Pharisees who were apparently active in this area where otherwise the influence of the Essenes was strongest. The rabbinical school of the Pharisees and Essenes had different views about marriage. The Pharisees consented to the man's writing a letter of divorce if he felt thus inclined. The Essenes emphasized monogamy with no possibility of marrying a second time. This was, then, a controversial subject in that region.

On the way to Batanea

The Pharisees resorted to Jesus to establish his position. They emphasized that Moses (cf. Dt 24:1) had allowed men to issue a letter of divorce and to send the wife away (Mk 10:1-9). In an authoritative declaration Jesus supports rather the attitude of the Essenes: *"Therefore what God has joined together, let man not put asunder"* (Mk 10:9).

Mark continues: *"When they were in the house again, the disciples asked Jesus about this"* (Mk 10:10).

Which house is meant? It is quite clear to me that although the warm summer months by the lake made it possible for Jesus to spend the nights outdoors, e.g., at the Eremos-cave, he and his friends needed a roof over their heads during the winter months, especially on the high plateau of the Batanea. Here we may entertain an idea about whom he stayed with in Batanea...

One possibility is that he might have stayed with his relatives in Kochaba. We know that Natzoreans were living there later on, for Julius Africanus had found out that it was there the people had kept the Davidic genealogies. Whether they already lived there at the time of Jesus is not certain but it seems very likely.

There is yet another fascinating possibility: the country home of the sisters, Mary and Martha. In this case the event which Luke alone records of Jesus' visit to the sisters (Lk 10:38-42) took place not in Bethany near Jerusalem but earlier in Bethany beyond the Jordan. According to Luke the event seems in fact to have taken place somewhere up in the North. Martha, the hostess, went to a lot of trouble to host Jesus and his followers. But it was the contemplative Mary who *"had chosen the better part"* (Lk 10:42). If we try to reconstruct the events we may imagine that the sisters, having heard of the condition of their brother Lazarus, whom they had left behind in Bethany near Jerusalem, hurried there ahead of Jesus. This would explain how they knew of Jesus' hiding place when they sent him the message *"Lord, the one you love is sick"* (Jn 11:3).

If we read the passages that follow and consider the landscape where Jesus' words were spoken, they appear in a very different light. We know that there were also Essene monks living in that neighborhood, pious Jews who observed celibacy so as to serve God more freely. In his reply to the remark of his disciples on marriage and divorce, he might well have been referring to those ascetics. *"Jesus replied, 'Not everyone can accept this word, but only those to whom it has been given. For some are eunuchs because they were born that way; others were made that way by men; and others have renounced marriage because of the kingdom of heaven. The one who can accept this should accept it'"* (Mt 19:11-12).

Mark and Matthew report another, lovely event. One senses how carefree and untroubled Jesus must have felt there.
"People were bringing little children to Jesus to have him touch them, but the disciples rebuked them. When Jesus saw this, he was indignant. He said to them, 'Let the little children come to me, and do not hinder them, for the kingdom of God belongs to such as these. I tell you the truth, anyone who will not receive the kingdom of God like a little child will never enter it.' And he took the children in his arms, put his hands on them and blessed them" (Mk 10:13-16).

4. THE LAST STAGE: UP TO JERUSALEM

After Lazarus' death, Jesus left Judea beyond the Jordan, either to go to Bethany on the eastern slope of the Mount of Olives as John's Gospel has it, or to go to Jerusalem via Jericho as noted by Mark and Matthew. At Bethphage and Bethany on the Mount of Olives (Mk 11:1) he mounted a donkey and rode in a triumphal procession into the city. If we follow John's chronology several events intervened between his arrival on the Mount of Olives and the festal entry: the resurrection of Lazarus (Jn 11:1-44), the banning of Jesus' activity by the Sanhedrin (Jn 11:47-52), Jesus' hiding in the village of Ephraim (present-day Taibeh) on the edge of the desert (Jn 11:54) and the anointing in Bethany (Jn 12:1-9). Only then, according to John's Gospel, followed the messianic entrance into the Holy City. All these events are chronologically feasible and in no way contradict the Synoptics.

113

The journey from Bethany in Batanea to Bethany near Jerusalem may have lasted four days. We may draw this conclusion from an observation by John. When Jesus had announced the death of Lazarus (Jn 11:14) he left and *"on his arrival, Jesus found that Lazarus had already been in the tomb for four days"* (Jn 11:17). This is the length of time it takes to walk from Batanea through the Jordan Valley to Bethany. In the heat of summer walking there is almost unbearable. In winter, though, this route is most agreeable. The whole desert would now have been green with colorful banks of flowers covering the ground which, during the dry summer months, would have looked arid and unfriendly.

Through this array of flowers Jesus may have passed on his journey up to Jerusalem. He wanted to arrive there before the Passover Festival. He and his followers probably spent the first night either in Pella or in Beth Shean. For the second night he could easily have found shelter in one of the many caves at the foot of the Samaritan mountains and on the third night he may have been the guest of Zacchaeus, the tax collector in Jericho.

Some of the caves at the foot of the Samaritan mountains where pilgrims found shelter

During his stay in Batanea Jesus must have made a deep impression on one nobleman who could have met him before Jesus went down into the Yarmuk valley. The young man fell to his knees and asked: *"Good teacher, what must I do to inherit eternal life?"* (Mk. 10:17). He had observed the commandments from childhood on but invited by Jesus to leave everything behind and to follow him, he lacked the courage to do so. *"He went away sad, because he had great wealth"* (Mk 10:22).

The Master was once again alone with his disciples. Jesus walked on ahead courageously. However, a sharp sense of anxiety hung over his followers (cf. Mk 10:32). He had referred twice already to the suffering awaiting him in Jerusalem. The first occasion had been at the foot of Mount Hermon in Caesarea Philippi. His words then met with stiff opposition from the apostles. The second occasion was on their return to Galilee on the borders of Lake Semachonitis (Hula). There they no longer dared to make any comment but they still could not understand him. Now he had called them together again. Perhaps they were sitting around a camp fire in front of one of the many caves in the Jordan valley that served Jerusalem pilgrims and travelers as shelters since earliest times. Now they heard the disturbing news for a third time in more detail:

> *"'We are going up to Jerusalem,' he said, 'and the Son of Man will be betrayed to the chief priests and teachers of the law. They will condemn him to death and will hand him over to the Gentiles, who will mock him and spit on him, flog him and kill him. Three days later he will rise'"* (Mk 10:33-34).

Whatever he encountered on his way after leaving Galilee, whether the colorful variety of people who were mixed together in the autonomous region of Batanea, or the happy throng of children crowding around him, or the valleys and meadows filled with flowers, the one thing he always had before his eyes was "This is my last journey. This journey takes me to Jerusalem and to my death."

At some distance from Jesus and the apostles, the women of Galilee were following, forming a separate caravan, as was the custom. Luke (8:2) enumerates the women that had been disciples of Jesus: *"Mary called Magdalene..., Johanna, the wife of Chuza, Susanna and several others, who had provided them with their own resources."* There was Mary, the mother of Jesus and foster mother of James and Josy and Salome, the wife of Zebedee and mother of James and John (cf. Mk 15:40). *"These used to follow him and look after him when he was in Galilee. And there were many other women who had come up to Jerusalem with him"* (Mk 15:49).

These two groups of pilgrims *"were on their way up to Jerusalem, with Jesus leading the way; and the disciples were in a daze, while those who followed were afraid"* (Mk 10:32).

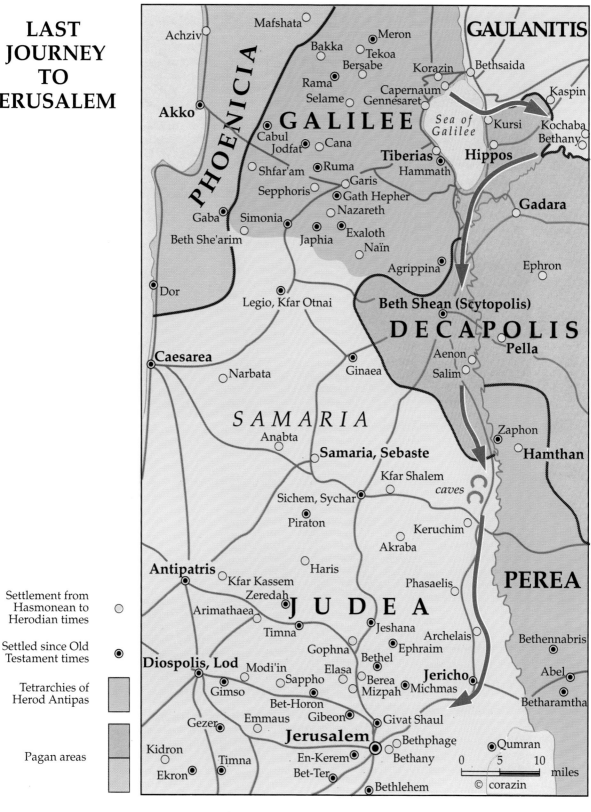

LAST JOURNEY TO JERUSALEM

GAULANITIS

Mafshata
Achziv
Bakka
Meron
Tekoa
Bersabe
Korazin
Bethsaida
Kaspin
Rama
Capernaum
Selame
Gennesaret
Kochaba
Akko
GALILEE
Sea of Galilee
Bethany
Cabul
Cana
Kursi
Jodfat
Ruma
Tiberias
Hippos
Garis
Hammath
Shfar'am
Gath Hepher
Gadara
Sepphoris
Nazareth
Gaba
Simonia
Exaloth
Beth She'arim
Japhia
Naïn
Ephron
Agrippina
Dor
Beth Shean (Scytopolis)
Legio, Kfar Otnai
DECAPOLIS
Pella
Caesarea
Ginaea
Aenon
Narbata
Salim
SAMARIA
Zaphon
Anabta
Hamthan
Samaria, Sebaste
Kfar Shalem
caves
Sichem, Sychar
Piraton
Keruchim
Akraba
Antipatris
Haris
Phasaelis
PEREA
Kfar Kassem
Zeredah
J U D E A
Jeshana
Arimathaea
Archelais
Bethennabris
Timna
Gophna
Ephraim
Diospolis, Lod
Modi'in
Bethel
Abel
Elasa
Berea
Jericho
Sappho
Mizpah
Michmas
Betharamtha
Gimso
Bet-Horon
Gibeon
Givat Shaul
Gezer
Emmaus
Jerusalem
Bethphage
Qumran
Kidron
Bethany
En-Kerem
Timna
Ekron
Bet-Ter
Bethlehem

PHOENICIA

Settlement from Hasmonean to Herodian times ○

Settled since Old Testament times ◉

Tetrarchies of Herod Antipas

Pagan areas

0   5   10   miles

© corazin

*Through this array of flowers
Jesus passed on his journey up
to Jerusalem.* Olive trees in
Jerusalem on the colored
spring-time carpet

EPILOGUE

This book is an attempt to see Jesus' life and work in Galilee as a whole through the eyes of Mark the Evangelist. Placed within the Fifth Gospel of the geographical setting and contemporary history, a rounded picture is offered instead of single pericopes, normally presented in isolation.

My long experience with Galilee and its landscape has helped me to set biblical events in particular places. I feel justified in doing so, for one reason, because of the conclusive results of archaeological excavations in the last twenty years (Nazareth, Magdala, Capernaum, Tabgha, Gennesaret, Bethsaida, Kursi, Caesarea Philippi). These settings are sometimes based on traditions that can be traced back to Byzantine times (such as Tabor or Hermon, the place of the healing of the woman with a hemorrhage, the ›Dodekathronos‹ on Tel Hadar). They are, at other times, based on detailed studies (Tabgha as Magadan-Dalmanutha, the sermon by the lake, Batanea as Bethany beyond the Jordan). Conjecture, too, is used to locate events, such as the place of healing of the blind man outside Bethsaida). Absolute certainty is not always obtainable, since the gospels were not intended to be guidebooks. However, this is not the point. What we are really trying to find are points of reference where one can best meditate on a particular event in the life of Jesus: where does it make sense, where could it most likely have happened?

Though I have in general taken Mark as a basis, I tried sometimes to fill in or complete the picture with information from the Gospel of John. Perhaps those who feel strongly about methodology may find some grounds here for criticism. But apart from a strongly divergent coloring of the two Gospels, I am convinced that Mark and John offer an excellent topographical and historical background of events in Galilee. I find that they do complement each other.

There is, for example, the difficult problem: was there one or were there two Feedings of the Multitude? A thorough examination of Mark's text (above ch 5 par 2) and the very old local tradition at Tabgha (Egeria) have convinced me that the First Feeding must have taken place on the western shore of the Sea of Galilee not too far from Capernaum. John wanted to include only one Feeding among his ›Seven Signs‹ (semeya), so he put together elements of both synoptic stories, e.g., the eastern shore is taken from the Second Feeding, the number of loaves and baskets from the First Feeding, etc.). By transposing the Feeding to the eastern shore, John must record Jesus as walking on the sea in an east-west direction. But the meeting with the disciples in the boat is once again at the traditional site in the west between Capernaum and the village Gennesaret. I find similar possibilities of completing the picture of the last area of Jesus' ministry in ›Judea beyond the Jordan‹ (see ch 7 par 2) which corresponds well with ›Bethany (or Batanea) beyond the Jordan‹ (Jn 1:12; 10:40).

Perhaps I have become too deeply part of this country to allow myself to be tied down by too exacting academic methodology. Along with the orientals I think in a different way from those whose learning is from schoolbooks.

We do have in this land an advantage which has been denied to Christian scholars in the past. We are a Christian minority in a Jewish majority. This was the situation of the primitive Church. This was the historical setting when the Gospels were written. It gives us a new perception of the Jewish way of thinking. Jesus was a Jew and so were the first believers. As a Jew, Jesus was shaped by his people and by the various aspects of life in his homeland. This was the milieu God's Son chose in order to share our human destiny. These were the surroundings in which Jesus grew to maturity and assumed his mission as the One sent by God. *"He grew in wisdom and stature, and in favor with God and men"* (Lk 2:52). Born with a truly human nature, Jesus learned through experience, and in prayers, the path he was to take through our world. He tried again and again, he left one path and took another, he closed himself to some and opened himself to others. In sharing a human life his divine nature became inseparably united with his human nature; this mutual intermingling was a living process which reached its peak and perfection only in his death and resurrection.

During these years in this land, I have come to know Jesus especially as a man, a man who had to struggle against as many odds, if not far more than I do. I appreciate him now as my brother who travelled, as I do, the rugged path of human life. The personality of this God-Man always and evermore fascinates me. When I walk along the banks of the Sea of Gennesaret I see him walking toward me from out of the early morning mist or from the play of colors in the setting sun. I have learned to deeply love this man from Galilee, the man whose footsteps crisscross mine day by day here in his preferred retreat of Ma-gadan.

Two thousand years ago when the Fifth Gospel was being etched into this land, two young men came to Jesus with the question, "Rabbi (which means Teacher) where do you live?" He replied,"Come and see" (Jn 1:39). Jesus renews this invitation to you. For you, too, it can bring intimate knowledge of the Natzorean Rabbi, as you journey with Jesus through the Galilee according to the Fifth Gospel.

I wonder, whether, through our common journeys throughout Galilee with this Natzorean Rabbi, I did succeed in passing on such affection to others, as well. Come and meet him yourself in this country which bore him!

Learn to read the Fifth Gospel!

Magdala

Valley of the Doves

Plain of Ginnosar

Place of ancient Gennesaret

Tel Kinnerot

Sea of Galilee

Tabgha -
Basilica and
Monastery

Dalmanutha

Church of Mensa Christi

Parking

Eremos

"Now as he walked by the sea of Galilee, he saw Simon and Andrew his brother casting their nets into the sea for they were fishermen" (Mk 1:16).

NOTES

BIBLE QUOTATIONS

Joshua: **3:10** p. 44. Isaiah: **8:23** p. 17; **11:1** p. 14; **14:19** p. 14; **49:6** p.78; **60:61** p. 55 Daniel: **7:25** p. 63

Matthew: **2:23** p. 13,14 ; **4:12-14** p. 28,29; **4:25** p. 39; **5:3-10** p. 38; **5:43f** p. 40; **7:29** p. 39; **11:20f** p. 34, 103; **14:28-31** p. 74; **15:21.22** p. 77; **15:24** p. 78; **15:29-31** p. 80; **15:32** p. 81; **16:22** p. 90; **19:2** p. 109; **19:11-12** p. 113

Mark: **1:9** p. 13; **1:15** p. 32; **1:17** p. 31; **1:18** p. 32; **1:27** p. 102; **1:37** p. 39; **3:21** p.59; **3:33f** p. 50; **3:6** p. 104; **4:1f** p. 41; **4:35** p. 42; **4:39** p. 43; **5:1** p. 43; **5:11** p. 44; **5:14** p. 44; **5:20** p. 45; **5:23** p. 46; **5:24-27** p. 47; **5:31-34** p. 47; **5:43** p. 48; **6:3** p. 50; **6:12** p. 69; **6:31f** p. 69; **6:34-35** p. 70; **6:41-44** p. 72; **6:45-46** p. 73; **6:47-50** p. 74; **6:52** p. 77; **6:54** p. 75; **7:15.19** p.76; **7:24.27.28** p. 77; **7:29.31** p. 78; **7:37** p. 79; **8:3** p. 81; **8:13-14** p. 88; **8:15** p. 90; **8:17-21** p. 89-90; **8:22-25** p. 94; **8:27.29** p. 95; **8:30.33** p. 96; **9:3** p. 97; **9:12** p. 99; **9:30** p. 98; **9:32-34.39** p. 99; **9:35** p. 100; **10:1** p. 109; **10:8.10** p. 112; **10:13-16** p.114; **10:17.22** p. 115; **10:32-34** p. 116

Luke: **1:34** p. 51; **2:30.32** p. 78; **2:52** p. 121; **3:3** p. 19; **3:14** p. 21; **7:5.9** p. 36; **4:22** p. 59; **4:24.30-31** p. 60; **13:31-33** p. 103

John: **1:14** p. 9; **1:41** p. 93; **2:11.12** p. 22; **2:14** p. 49; **2:23** p. 61; **2:24-25** p. 62; **3:21-26** p. 27-28; **3:30** p. 27; **4:1-4** p. 23; **4:42.43.45** p. 24; **6:6** p. 71; **6:14f** p. 73; **6:51.52.55.60.66-68** p. 88; **7:2-5** p. 61; **7:6-9** p. 63; **7:37-38** p. 64; **10:40-42** p. 120; **11:3** p. 113; **11:17** p. 114; **19:26f** p. 64

Acts: **1:14** p.49; **10:37f** p 101 Hebrews: **5:8-9** p. 121 1. Corinthians: **15:3** p. 65

GALILEAN TIMECHART

B.C. 1225	° Tribe of Naphtali at Lake Kinneret ° Tribe of Zebulon in the mountains	Josh. 19:10-16; 19:32-39
B.C. 873-853	° Ahab, King in Samaria of Northern Kingdom ° The prophets Elijah and Elisha	1K 16:29-22:40
B.C. 733	° Conquest by Tiglath-Pileser (745-727 vChr) Assyrian exile. ° Galilee incorporated into Assyrian empire as the Province Megiddo. 600 years as ›Galilee of the Gentiles‹	2K 15:29 Is 8:23
B.C. 163	° Campaign of Simeon the Maccabee in Galilee, to rescue the Jewish population from annihilation. Transfer of the rescued to the Jewish heartland of Judea	1 M 5:21-23
B.C. 104	° Incorporation of Galilee into the Hasmonean kingdom by Aristobulus (104-103); Compulsory Judaizing of the gentile population and a marked return of Jews from Babylon and Persia.	Jos. Flav.: Ant. 13,318
ca. B.C. 100	° (?) Return of the Davidic clan of Natzoreans from exile; Initial settlement in Kochaba (Batanea), and shortly after in Nazareth	Cf. Eusebius, Hist. Eccl. 1,7,14
B.C. 63	° Pompey founds hellenistic union of cities of the Decapolis.	B.J. 3,446
B.C. 47	° Herod becomes the territorial ruler of Galilee ° Execution of Ezekhias of Gamla	Ant. 14,158-160
B.C. 40(37)-4	° Herod the Great becomes King of all Judea, including Galilee, Batanea and the Decapolis	Ant. 14,144; 14,385 B.J. 1,282
B.C. (?) 25	° Birth of Mary in Jerusalem	Protevangelium

18 B.C.	° Herod begins to enlarge the Temple	Ant. 15,380 B.J. 1,401
ca. 8 B.C.	° Betrothal of Mary to the Davidic Joseph from Nazareth	Protevangelium Mt 1,18
7(6) B.C.	° Birth of Jesus in Bethlehem	Mt 1:18-25 Lk 2:1-7
4 B.C.	° Death of Herod the Great and partition of his kingdom among his three sons: Archelaus (Judea), Herod Antipas (Galilee and Perea), Philip (Gaulanitis, Batanea, Trachonitis)	Ant. 17,319 B.J. 2,94
4 B.C. - A.D. 6	° Unsettled rule of Archelaus	Ant. 17,342 B.J. 22,11
A.D. 1 (?)	° Joseph and Mary go with Jesus to Nazareth	Mt 2:22
A.D. 6	° Census by Quirinius ° Foundation of the Zealot party by Jehuda of Gamla and the Pharisee Tzadok ° 12 yr old Jesus becomes Bar-Mitzva in Jerusalem	Ant. 18,4; 9,23-25 B.J. 2,118 Acts 5:37 Lk 2:41ff
A.D. 28-30	Public ministry of Jesus (see separate Timechart)	
A.D. 34	° Death of Philip the Tetrarch. He was buried in the mausoleum built by him in Bethsaida-Julias	Ant. 18,106
A.D. 36	° Defeat of the army of Antipas in war against the Nabateans.	Ant. 18,116-119
A.D. 37	° Agrippa becomes king in the territory of the deceased Philip.	B.J. 2,181
A.D. 38	° Exile of Antipas the Tetrarch to Spain. Agrippa I becomes king in Galilee as well, and in A.D. 41 over the whole territory once ruled by Herod the Great.	Ant. 2,181-183 Ant. 18,237
A.D. 44	° Death of Agrippa I in Caesarea Maritima	Ant. 19,350 Apg 12,23
A.D. 50-100	° Agrippa II, King of Galilee, Gaulanitis and Batanea	Ant. 20,138
A.D. 66-70	° The great revolt of the Jewish population under the Zealots against Rome. Flavius Josephus leads the war in Galilee and is taken prisoner. The siege of Gamla ends with the collective suicide of its inhabitants.	B.J. 2,568; 3,384-398; 4,62-83

TIMECHART OF JESUS' PUBLIC MINISTRY
TOWARDS A CHRONOLOGY

The years 26/27/28	• Public ministry of John the Baptist in the area of the Jordan river	Mk 1:4; Lk 3:2f
January 28	• Baptism of Jesus in the Jordan river near Jericho; • 40 Days in the Desert	Mk 1:9.12
March 28	John is baptizing in Batanea in a tributary of the Jordan river, the Kerith (Yarmuk). Jesus is introduced to disciples of John at Bethany beyond the Jordan. Jesus goes with his first disciples to the Wedding at Cana.	Jn 1:28-2,2
March 28	Jesus stays with family and disciples for a time in Capernaum.	Jn 2:12
April 28	• Passover in Jerusalem. The Cleansing of the Temple draws attention to Jesus from Essene groups, as well as the Galilean Pharasee, Nicodemus. Jesus does not rely on these people.	Jn 2:13-3:1-21
Summer 28	Jesus preaches and his disciples baptize in Judea. John baptizes by the springs of Aenon near Salim, south of Beth-Shean.	Jn 3:22-23
Autumn 28	John stands up against Herod Antipas and is thrown into prison. Jesus returns via Samaria to Galilee.	Mt 14:3f Mk 6:17 Jn 4:1f
Nov 28	With the **Arrest of John** Jesus begins his own mission.	Mt 4:12
Nov 28	Jesus finds two pairs of brothers, Simon and Andrew, James and John, while they were fishing at Tabgha (Ma-gadan) and calls them to become disciples.	Mt 4:18ff; Mk 1:16ff
Winter 28/29	• The beginning in Capernaum • Preaching in neighboring villages; News of his miracles and his message spreads. • Choosing of the Twelve	Mk 1:21ff
Jan./Feb. 29	Large crowds at the sermon on the Mount and while preaching at the Bay of Parables	Mt 4:23-5,1ff; Mk 4:1ff

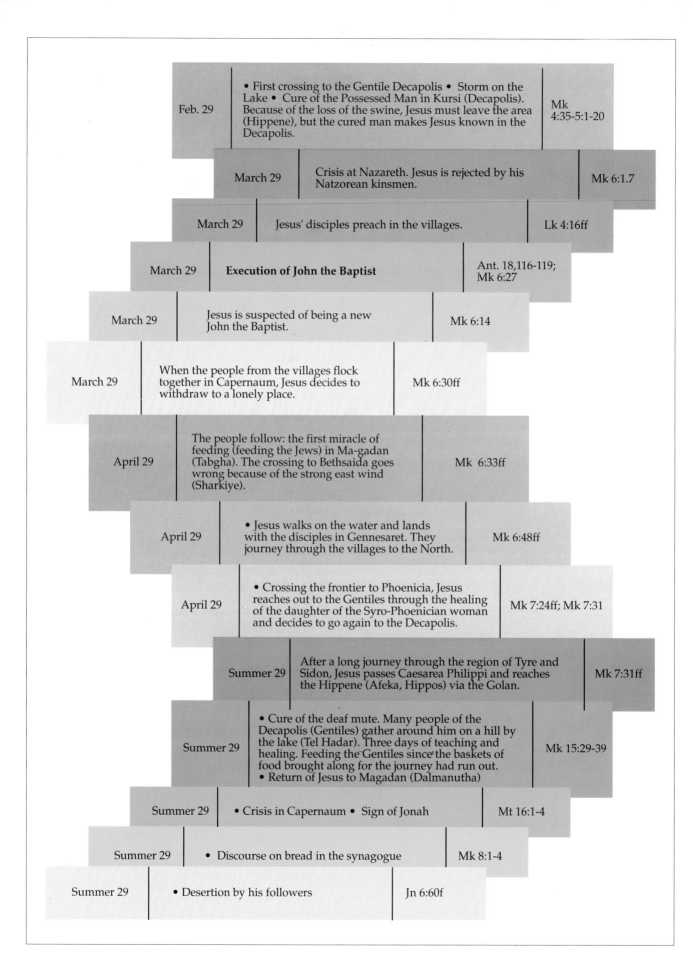

Feb. 29	• First crossing to the Gentile Decapolis • Storm on the Lake • Cure of the Possessed Man in Kursi (Decapolis). Because of the loss of the swine, Jesus must leave the area (Hippene), but the cured man makes Jesus known in the Decapolis.	Mk 4:35-5:1-20
March 29	Crisis at Nazareth. Jesus is rejected by his Natzorean kinsmen.	Mk 6:1.7
March 29	Jesus' disciples preach in the villages.	Lk 4:16ff
March 29	**Execution of John the Baptist**	Ant. 18,116-119; Mk 6:27
March 29	Jesus is suspected of being a new John the Baptist.	Mk 6:14
March 29	When the people from the villages flock together in Capernaum, Jesus decides to withdraw to a lonely place.	Mk 6:30ff
April 29	The people follow: the first miracle of feeding (feeding the Jews) in Ma-gadan (Tabgha). The crossing to Bethsaida goes wrong because of the strong east wind (Sharkiye).	Mk 6:33ff
April 29	• Jesus walks on the water and lands with the disciples in Gennesaret. They journey through the villages to the North.	Mk 6:48ff
April 29	• Crossing the frontier to Phoenicia, Jesus reaches out to the Gentiles through the healing of the daughter of the Syro-Phoenician woman and decides to go again to the Decapolis.	Mk 7:24ff; Mk 7:31
Summer 29	After a long journey through the region of Tyre and Sidon, Jesus passes Caesarea Philippi and reaches the Hippene (Afeka, Hippos) via the Golan.	Mk 7:31ff
Summer 29	• Cure of the deaf mute. Many people of the Decapolis (Gentiles) gather around him on a hill by the lake (Tel Hadar). Three days of teaching and healing. Feeding the Gentiles since the baskets of food brought along for the journey had run out. • Return of Jesus to Magadan (Dalmanutha)	Mk 15:29-39
Summer 29	• Crisis in Capernaum • Sign of Jonah	Mt 16:1-4
Summer 29	• Discourse on bread in the synagogue	Mk 8:1-4
Summer 29	• Desertion by his followers	Jn 6:60f

September 29	• Feast of Tabernacles in Jerusalem (?)	Jn 7:2ff

October 29	**• Journey North: Instruction of apostles.**	Mk 8:13-9:33

October 29	• Crossing from Capernaum to Bethsaida	Mk 8:13-21

October 29	• Cure of the blind man (symbolic healing)	Mk 8:22-26

October 29	• Journey to Caesarea Philippi • Peter confesses Jesus as the Messiah • Correction of the disciples' messianic aspirations • First prediction of the Passion; tension	Mk 8:27-33

October 29	• Transfiguration on the High Mountain	Mk 9:2ff

October 29	• Cure of the epileptic young man	Mk 9:14-29

October 29	• Return to Galilee • Second prediction of the Passion	Mk 9:30-32

October 29	• Return to Capernaum	Mk 9:33

November 29	Warning: threat of danger from Herod Antipas	Lk 13:31ff

November 29	Jesus leaves Galilee.	Mt 19:11

November 29	The group travels to *Judea on the other side of the Jordan* (Batanea). [Or first they go to the feast of Hanukkah to Jerusalem and then on to Batanea]	Mk 10:1; Jn 10:22f. 40-42

Winter 29/30	• In Batanea. Further activity in the territory of Philip unhindered by threat of violence.	Mk 10:1; Joh 10:42

Winter 29/30	• Discourse on marriage and eunuchs for the sake of the kingdom of God	Mk 10:2ff

Winter 29/30	• Jesus and the children	Mk 10:13-16

Winter 29/30	• Jesus is guest at the home of Mary and Martha (?)	Lk 10:38ff

Winter 29/30	• The rich young man	Mk 10:17f

Feb./March 30	Jesus travels along the Jordan valley. Third prediction of the Passion. Jesus goes on to Jericho with the Twelve and then up to Jerusalem.	Mk 10:32ff
April 30	• Death and Resurrection of Jesus	
April/May 30	• Appearances of Jesus in Galilee – on the lakeside and on the mountain near Capernaum. This last appearance on the Eremos Heights was probably also the occasion when *he appeared to five hundred brethren at one time*	Mk 14:28; 16:7; Mt 28:16ff; Jn 21:1ff; 1Cor 15:6

EVIDENCE FOR THE CHRONOLOGY OF JESUS' PUBLIC MINISTRY

(according to Mark,
with additional support from Johannine data)

1.

THREE PASSOVER FEASTS IN JOHN'S GOSPEL

a. Passover while John the Baptist was still alive (Jn 2:13;23) in the year 28. Luke mentions that the Baptist appeared in the 15th year of the hegemonia (i.e., actual reign) of the Emperor Tiberius (Lk 3:1) in the whole region of Jordan (Lk 3:3; Jn 1:28; 3:23) as a wandering preacher. That means 26/27. The first Johannine Passover would therefore have been in 28. This is consistent with the objection made by the people: *"It has taken forty-six years to build this temple, and you are going to raise it in three days?"* (Jn 2:20) 18 B.C. is generally taken to be the start of the Temple building by Herod: 18 + 28 = 46.

b. Passover at the time of the first miracle of feeding
(Jn 6:4) in the year 29.

c. Passover at the time of the Passion (Jn 13:1) in the year 30.

2.

VEGETATION

a. A herd of swine can find pasture on the hillside over the Lake only between February and April (cf. Mk 5:11).

b. First Miracle of Feeding (April 29): they sat down in groups on green grass (Mk 6:37; Jn 6:10).

c. Second Miracle of Feeding (Summer 29): the grass had died off in the meantime and the 4000 sat down on the earth or on stones (cf. Mk 8:6).

d. Journey through the cornfields (Mk 2:23, Mt 12:1) and the rubbing of the ears of corn must have been in May/June, perhaps during the journey from the Lake into the neighborhood of Tyre.

3.

WINDS

Different winds blow over the Lake at different times of the year. In the summer the afternoon west wind (Gharbiyeh) cools off the intense summer heat somewhat, but causes no storms.

In winter and spring the east wind (Sharkiyeh) can be dangerous, and often results in sudden storms.

a. The Storm on the Lake – Feb 29 (cf Mk 4:35-41).

b. The strong contrary east wind prevented the disciples from reaching the appointed destination of Bethsaida at the mouth of the Jordan, in spite of hard rowing – March/April 29. *"He saw the disciples straining at the oars, because the wind was against them"* (Mk 6:48).

4.

CLIMATE

For the pilgrimage to Jerusalem three or four days were needed. In general, pilgrims followed the Jordan valley only during the cool season. In summer, because of the almost unbearable heat in the valley, travellers followed the mountain route, in spite of the dangers that Samaritans posed.

a. In Winter 28 Jesus walked through the valley to John the Baptist, who was baptizing near Jericho. (This is also the traditional liturgical date in Eastern and Western Churches for the Baptism of Jesus.)

b. Jesus travelled home from Jerusalem through Samaria – Oct. 28 (cf. Jn 4:3-4).

c. Final journey of Jesus to Jerusalem through Jericho – February-March 30 (cf. Mk 10:48).

5.

FISHING

In the cool months fishermen of Capernaum throw their nets near the beach of Tabgha, where once there was a small harbor (Peter's harbor). The Tilapias (›Peter's fish‹) being a tropical species suffer from the winter cold. Attracted by water from the warm springs at Tabgha (Seven Springs), large shoals of this type of fish gather in the area. In winter and spring heavy catches can be made.

a. Call of the disciples – Nov 28. The sons of Zebedee and Jonas formed a partnership. They had come, together with the hired laborers, from fishing on the open water to land. While the one group got the nets ready for the next expedition, Peter and Andrew attempted to catch some more fish in the shallow water with their casting nets. Jesus went past and called them (cf. Mk 1:16-20).

b. Appearance of Jesus after the Resurrection on the shore of Tabgha – April/May 30. The plentiful haul of fish (cf. Jn 21:1ff).

TABGHA

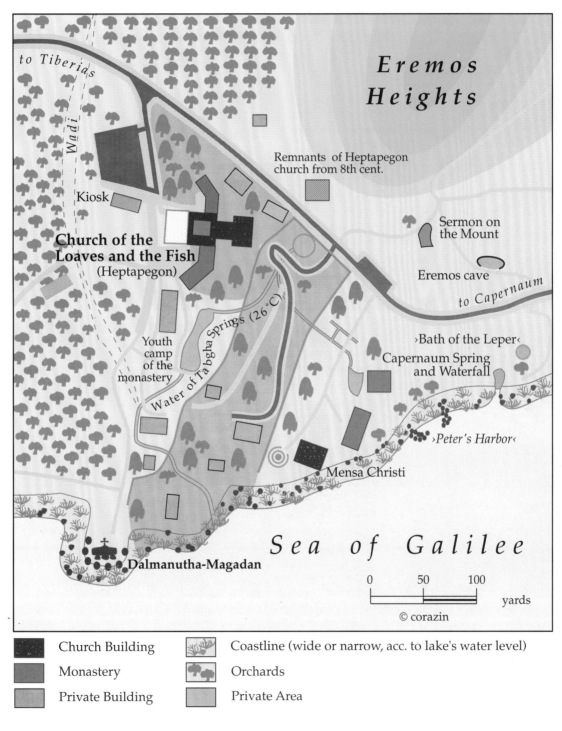

to Tiberias

Wadi

Eremos Heights

Kiosk

Remnants of Heptapegon church from 8th cent.

Church of the Loaves and the Fish (Heptapegon)

Sermon on the Mount

Eremos cave

to Capernaum

Youth camp of the monastery

Water of Tabgha Springs (26°C)

›Bath of the Leper‹

Capernaum Spring and Waterfall

›Peter's Harbor‹

Mensa Christi

Dalmanutha-Magadan

Sea of Galilee

0   50   100

yards

© corazin

■	Church Building	
■	Monastery	
■	Private Building	

	Coastline (wide or narrow, acc. to lake's water level)	
	Orchards	
	Private Area	

LIST OF PHOTOS

ILLUSTRATIONS

BOXES

THE LAND OF
GALILEE
THAT
JESUS WALKED

Legend:

- Settlement mentioned in the OT
- Settlement at the time of Jesus
- Settled since OT times and earlier
- Roman road
- Harbor or anchorage
- Hellenistic city
- Predominantly gentile areas. **Phoenicia** was incorporated 63 BC into the Roman Empire, while the cities of the **Decapolis** were severed from the Hasmonean Kingdom and given the status of Hellenistic cities.
- Where Jesus preached and healed
- Routes frequented by Jesus
- Early Christian community
- Church from later periods
- Fortified AD 66 by Flavius Josephus in the revolt against Rome
- Captured AD 67 by Roman army

Map labels:

House of the Centurion

Capernaum

›His own town‹ Mt 9:1

Tax office of Matthew
Mk 2:14

Healing of the
Hemorrhoissa, Mk 5:25

Sermon from the Boat, Mk 4:1

Via Maris

A strong wind was blowing
and the waters grew rough.
Jn 6:18

Chapel and Hospice of the Beatitudes

Sermon of the
Beatitudes

Eremos-
Grotto

›Harbor of Peter‹

Jesus transfers to Peter the
care of his flock. Joh 21:17

Mk 6:51

Mensa Christi

Ma-gadan (Dalmanutha)

Heptapegon (Tabgha)

Feeding of the Multitude,
Mt 14:20

Gennesaret

Kinneret

Enlargement of the northern lake's shore

Galilean Journeys of Jesus

First Journey (Mk 4:35-5:21)   Second Journey (Mk 6:31-8:10)   Third Journey (Mk 8:13-9:33)